W9-AKW-801

Beyond the Call of Duty

BERNIE FISHER, UNITED STATES AIR FORCE

The Story of an American Hero in Vietnam

Beyond the Call of Duty

Colonel Bernard Fisher
USAF Retired

and Jerry Borrowman

Special thanks to Marcella Borrowman and Hilary Borrowman for their editorial comments and suggestions.

Visit us at shadowmountain.com

Library of Congress Cataloging-in-Publication Data

Fisher, Bernard, 1927–

Beyond the call of duty : the story of an American hero in Vietnam / Bernard Fisher, Jerry Borrowman.

p. cm.

ISBN 1-59038-247-1 (hardbound : alk. paper)

1. Fisher, Bernard, 1927– 2. Vietnamese Conflict, 1961–1975—Personal narratives, American. 3. Vietnamese Conflict, 1961–1975—Aerial operations, American. 4. United States. Air Force—Officers—Biography. I. Borrowman, Jerry. II. Title.

DS559.5 .F52 2004
959.704'348'092—dc22 2003023925

Printed in the United States of America 72076
Publishers Printing, Salt Lake City, UT

10 9 8 7 6 5 4 3

To the men and women of the United States Armed Forces who willingly place their lives at risk to protect the freedoms of America and our allies twenty-four hours a day, all around the world. We hope this story will help you better understand their professional lives and the sacrifices they make on our behalf.

We also dedicate the book to Realla Fisher, Bernie's wife and companion for more than fifty-five years.

CONTENTS

PRELUDE

THE WHITE HOUSE

Washington, D.C., January 19, 1967

IN SOME WAYS, STANDING IN the Red Room of the White House waiting to meet the president made me more nervous than serving on active duty in Vietnam. We arrived in a black limousine that took us directly to the front portico of the executive mansion, and I sincerely looked forward to the events of the day. But now, as the ceremony was about to get under way, I found myself in a mental struggle wondering exactly how one addresses the president. The military aides assigned to help me and my family while in Washington had carefully laid out all the plans and alternatives for how we should proceed while standing in the glare of the public spotlight, but the aides had somehow missed this key point. Something in my mind told me I should call him "Mr. President," but for some reason that sounded funny, as if the phrase were used only in television sitcoms. As a major in the United States Air Force, I supposed it would be appropriate to simply call the commander-in-chief "Sir," but I just wasn't sure. Just then I caught the eye of the chief protocol officer, who came over to where I stood in line so I could whisper my problem into his ear. He smiled. Apparently I wasn't the only one to feel so out of place that I could forget such a basic title. He assured me that "Mr. President" was the appropriate response.

With that settled, I stepped back to my wife's side and relaxed as we tried to keep our five boys in some kind of a proper line. Everyone in the room was waiting in anticipation for the president to walk through the door—everyone, that is, but our youngest boy, Scotty, who was suffering from jet lag and ready for a nap. He slipped out of line, crawled up on one of the ornate davenports that had been part of former First Lady Jacqueline Kennedy's redecorating of the White House, snuggled in, and promptly curled up to fall asleep.

I smiled to myself, thinking that perhaps Scotty was the smartest among us, not getting caught up in the pageantry of the honors that would be bestowed on me and the members of my team that day. In many ways, I felt ambivalent about what was happening—we were simply professional airmen who had done our duty in Vietnam.

The rescue for which I was to be honored had taken place almost a year earlier, but it had taken this long to consider and act on the recommendation for the Congressional Medal of Honor. Two of the men involved in the rescue had previously been awarded the Silver Star, while the other two had each received the Distinguish Flying Cross. I was thrilled that they were joining us for my ceremony here in the White House. I could never have imagined on that cloudy day over Ashau Valley in Vietnam how much that day's events would change all of our lives.

There was a stirring in the room, which broke into my thoughts, and I turned to see the door fly open as an aide preceded President Lyndon B. Johnson through the doors. The president entered the room with a forceful stride and a commanding presence that seemed to dominate everything else in the room. He was an extremely tall man, particularly when compared to my five-foot-eight-inch height. He came up and saluted me, shook my hand, and asked me to introduce the members of my family.

"Mr. President, I'm pleased to introduce you to my wife, Realla."

He offered a handshake, and when Realla responded, her right hand completely disappeared in the grasp of his huge hand. I then introduced each of the four older boys, who stood respectfully in their suits. He chatted amiably with them for a few moments, helping everyone to relax. I didn't know exactly what to say about Scotty, but it turned out I didn't need to worry. The president spied him lying on the couch, not quite asleep, so he walked over and sat down next to him, talking quietly with him for a few moments until the little boy smiled.

Then the president stood up and asked, "Are you ready?"

I responded, "Yes, sir, I guess we are."

"Then let's go," he said enthusiastically, thumping me in the chest as he said it. He hit really hard. I was totally unprepared for that, and it about knocked the wind out of me, making me stagger a bit from the blow. But he didn't have time to notice, as he was already propelling me forward by the arm as members of the White House staff opened the doors to the corridor in front of us. We walked a few paces and made a sharp turn to the right to enter the much larger East Room of the White House. Passing through the door, I could see a line of dignitaries and guests, including my mother and other family members, flanked by a large contingent of reporters whose flash cameras were already doing their best to blind us. I drew in my breath as we started into the crowd, wondering to myself, "Just how did a boy who grew up on a twenty-acre farm in Clearfield, Utah, end up here?"

PART 1

Establishing a Military Career

CHAPTER ONE

SEAMAN FIRST CLASS

I DON'T KNOW EXACTLY WHEN my fascination with airplanes began. When I got old enough to have a paper route, I had to ride my bicycle on a five-mile route up the dirt road that led to Hill Air Force Base near my home in Clearfield, Utah, to deliver papers to families living on the base. I often stopped and watched the aircraft taking off and landing, trying to imagine how it felt to leave the ground and soar through the air.

I couldn't believe my good fortune when I actually had the chance to experience flight when I was thirteen years old. The adviser to our church's young men's organization was named Haven Barlow, and we kids loved him. He was young and single, and he could relate to a bunch of twelve- and thirteen-year-old boys. One day, a friend and I were teasing him about his girlfriend when he startled us with a question:

"Would you guys like to go flying in an airplane at the Ogden Airport?"

"Are you serious?"

"I'm serious if you'll let up on the teasing."

"Wow—that sounds like the greatest thing in the world!"

Airplanes were still pretty uncommon in 1940, and I didn't know anyone besides Haven who had been in one. The airplane he was authorized to fly was a single engine J-3C Piper Cub. I was surprised to find that they stored the planes tipped forward on their noses, with tails up in the air. This allowed them to stack the planes almost on top of each other to get more airplanes inside the protection of the hangar, and we had to move two or three out onto the tarmac to extract our plane. Haven climbed into the cockpit and checked a lot of instruments; then he fired up the engine and revved it until he was satisfied it was in proper condition to fly. The force of the propeller backwash was startling, prompting me to move back to a safer spot as Haven, with my friend Donald Jacobs, taxied out onto the runway and brought the aircraft into position for takeoff. With a roar, Haven brought the engine to full throttle, and they were off the ground and into the air. The sound of the engine faded quickly as they circled out and over the field, disappearing to the south while leaving me anxiously awaiting my turn.

It wasn't long before I heard the drone of the engine, and they coasted into a nice, easy landing. Donald climbed out of the passenger door with a big grin on his face, and in no time I found myself crawling up the strut and into the cramped little cabin. The airplane was different from anything I'd experienced before. The metal in the wing and the door seemed almost fragile, and even though it was a simple airplane, there were dozens of gauges and controls in the cockpit to raise my curiosity. As soon as Donald was clear, Haven pushed the throttle wide open, and the engine roared to life. The aircraft started trembling as it picked up ground speed, and I was amazed at how fast we accelerated. I loved the sensation of being forced back against the leather seat, and I found myself holding my breath. The noise and vibration increased, and then suddenly the sound changed, the vibrations quit, and the ground was falling away below me. That had to be the greatest feeling of my life. It took a few moments to get used to the side-to-side motion as we danced on the air currents, but before I could really think much about it, Haven banked hard and headed south toward Clearfield. As we gained altitude, the cars on the roads beneath us started to look like toys, and I was amazed to see what the roofs of familiar buildings looked like from this strange new vantage point. When we reached cruising altitude, it seemed like we were almost moving in slow motion because our point of reference was so different up there. Haven circled our farm and then headed back toward Ogden. I wished the ride could last forever, but gasoline was expensive, and even a Piper Cub went through it pretty fast.

Landing seemed pretty odd as we started to drift down to the ground. A small airplane tends to swagger in the wind as it loses altitude, and sometimes it looked like we were going to land at an angle to the runway rather than straight on. As we got closer and closer to the ground, the perception of speed increased, and when we hit the runway, I thought we were going way too fast to get stopped in time. I must have held my breath, because I let it out slowly as I felt the jerk of the wheels touching the ground. Haven pumped the brakes until we slowed down and came to a stop.

It was over, just like that, and unfortunately it would be years before I got to fly again. Probably the thing I liked best was how serene it felt to be detached from the earth. I'd never experienced such an exhilarating sense of freedom. I loved everything about that flight, and I went home and built a model airplane to remind me of it.

My interest in machines wasn't limited to airplanes. Even though I wasn't old enough to drive, I asked my dad if I could fix up a 1927 Chevy that my parents had abandoned to the barnyard several years earlier. The car had no roof, and a family of chickens was nesting in the front seat. I don't think my dad thought I could ever get it going, so he wasn't too worried giving me permission to try. After cleaning it up and working on the engine for a couple of months, I borrowed a battery from a neighbor and got the engine running. With a lot of work I finally got the old car off the cinder blocks and onto its own wheels. Even with my best efforts, though, it was still in terrible shape. The tires were so brittle that I had to wrap the inner-tubes with canvas to prevent blowouts.

I hadn't gotten around to fixing the brakes yet but decided to take some friends out for a test drive. As I came around a corner in the late dusk, I saw some movement up ahead, which turned out to be a herd of cattle. I was driving way too fast for the road, and with no brakes I hit a couple of cows. I expected the owner to turn me over to the police, but instead he was apologetic because he didn't have any lights on to indicate the herd was on the road. So there we were, each trying to apologize to the other, until it dawned on us that we were both in the wrong. We each went our own way, with me driving much more carefully than before. I felt bad about hurting the animals, but I was glad that none of my friends had been injured.

I wish I could say I slowed down after that, but I continued to drive pretty aggressively because I loved the sensation of acceleration and speed. A few years later, when I was driving legally, I'd worked to buy a '29 Ford convertible, one of the most enjoyable cars I've ever owned. I loved having my hands under the hood, and I worked tirelessly to get maximum performance out of the engine. One day, my friends and I were going down to Layton, Utah, from our home in Clearfield. It was a warm, sunny day, so we had the top down, and one of the guys was riding in the rumble seat. It felt so great to have the wind rushing past that I probably came into town a little too fast. I don't know if it was something I did or just a defect in the car, but one of the tires came loose and started rolling down the main street of Layton at a pretty high speed, fully detached from the car. My car hit the ground and started skidding around, leaving a blazing trail of sparks flying from where the hub of the wheel dragged on the street. We spun around right in the middle of Main Street, to the astonished looks of the people on the sidewalks. Meanwhile, the rogue tire bounced off a couple of cars before going airborne up and over a parked car right in front of Cowley's Drug Store. It was all pretty exciting, with no casualties except for some tire marks on a couple of cars, but the people in Layton were not at all amused. I got into trouble for that one, and I was relieved I didn't lose my license.

I hope it doesn't sound like I was a bad kid, because aside from a few incidents like those, I was a hardworking guy who did his best to help my family make it through the lean years of the Depression.

In the fall of 1941, I wasn't really paying a lot of attention to world affairs, except for the fact that Ab Jenkins and his "Mormon Meteor" were setting land-speed records out on the Bonneville Salt Flats just seventy miles west of where I lived. Each time he completed a time trial, I'd check out the times, calculate the speed, and dream about what driving that fast must be like. It took a lot of courage to drive that fast, when even the slightest mistake could send the vehicle reeling end-over-end, but the payoff in what they were learning about engine technology somewhat justified the risk. Ab was a real hero to me. Then December 7 arrived, and the world changed for all of us with the bombing of Pearl Harbor. I was about to turn fifteen years old when the attack occurred, so there was no immediate opportunity for me to go into military service. A lot of the older boys I knew at church dropped out of school or college so they could enlist. It was both exciting and ominous to think they were going off to battle.

The most immediate effect of the war in Clearfield was that the economy picked up. As the country started preparing to send soldiers into battle, government orders for goods and services went through the roof! I benefited from the new activity by getting a job as a forklift operator after school down at the Freeport Center loading naval ammunition onto railroad cars. The pay was good, and my family appreciated the financial help.

As I approached my senior year, the war became more and more of a reality in my life. When I turned seventeen, I decided to enlist so I could have some say over which branch of the military I'd serve in. My friend Donald Jacobs was two years older than I was, and at eighteen he'd enlisted in the Merchant Marines to serve on supply ships in the Pacific. Since he was one of the guys I looked up to, I decided to follow his example. Unfortunately, they told me the Merchant Marines had filled their quota, so that option wasn't available. I looked at the material the recruiting office had on hand and decided to try the Navy's V-5 program for training pilots. I signed up for the test but failed. I wanted to take it again, but they wouldn't let me. I felt frustrated but decided that I'd still like to join the Navy. Since I loved working on cars so much, I applied to become an aircraft mechanic. This time the Navy accepted me. I continued in high school until January 1945, when I reached my eighteenth birthday. Because so many of my classmates were signing up to defend our country, the school made special arrangements so we could qualify for early graduation.

Shortly after my birthday, I received official notification that I was to report to Fort Douglas in Salt Lake City for induction and processing, followed a short time later by a transfer to Boot Camp in Memphis, Tennessee. Since I'd never been east of Utah, I actually found that pretty exciting, and I looked forward to seeing the countryside on the train journey east. By this point in World War II, however, the Union Pacific Railroad was moving so many troops that they'd run out of passenger cars. To meet the demand, they simply converted old cattle cars into troop carriers by hosing out the cars and bolting in some wooden seats. There were no windows to look out of, just two days of staring at the inside of a wooden boxcar. Some of the taller men occasionally stood on tiptoes to look out through a set of slats in each corner, but the slats were beyond my reach. For me the trip wasn't as bad as it might have been, since a number of my friends from church had been assigned to the same car, and we were able to talk to each other and play games.

On our arrival in Memphis, we transferred by bus to the Navy Air Technical Training Center for boot camp, the purpose of which was to orient us to military life and toughen us up physically. Approximately half of each day was spent in classes learning military rank and insignia, proper protocol, and so forth, and the other half was spent in physical exercise, marching, and drills. I was in good enough shape from working on the farm and playing high school sports that I got along all right, but some of the men really suffered until they adapted. Like everyone else, I learned to make a bed with the corners so tightly tucked that you could bounce a quarter off the blanket when you were done. During the rare times we weren't in class or drill, we could "relax" by engaging in competitive sports, including boxing. Since I'd done some boxing back in Clearfield, I did pretty well in the boxing ring.

There was only one time I resented the Navy during boot camp, and that was when an officer gave me a hard time for a slight offense while standing in a drill line. We'd been marching around for more than an hour when one of the tactical officers came up and ordered us to stand at strict attention. I'd been carrying a rifle during the drills, and my hand was kind of numb, so I unconsciously wiggled my fingers a bit to restore blood flow. The officer saw this infraction out of the corner of his eye and seized on it as an opportunity to discipline me. He ordered me to hold the rifle over my head and run on a track that was nicknamed "the grinder." I could accept that I'd made a mistake and deserved punishment, but what he did next really infuriated me—he simply walked off without releasing me from the drill. Of course, there was no way to tell if he intended for me to stop, or if he was setting me up for even worse discipline if I stopped without permission, so I just kept running. After what seemed like an eternity, I simply couldn't hold my arms up any longer, and they started to sag from exhaustion. At that point the noncommissioned officer who was in charge of our group came over and told me to put the gun down and take five. The officer who'd ordered my discipline never even returned to check on me.

At the end of boot camp, I received orders to transfer to Norman, Oklahoma, for aircraft mechanics school, where my love of automobiles served me well. Our group progressed through the twenty-one weeks of the school at a pretty fair clip. By the end, we were disassembling and reassembling an F-4U Corsair assigned specifically for our training. The school also maintained some aircraft on the actual flight line, which they let us work on occasionally.

I learned an important lesson while working on the bomb bay doors of the aircraft. My assignment was to find and correct a problem in the hydraulic system. To complete the task, I had to get the bomb bay doors closed, but no matter what I tried, I couldn't find the trip-release to do it. I prodded and poked at various levers with a broom handle until one of the instructors noticed what I was doing. He issued a curt order for me to stand at attention, and then he said he wanted to show me something. I moved out of the bomb-well and watched as he used the broom handle to activate the correct release. The doors slammed shut with terrific force, sending a shudder through the entire frame of the aircraft. The doors were under 3,000 pounds of hydraulic pressure, and if I'd actually hit the correct release from where I was previously standing, I would have been crushed by the force of those massive doors. I was far more careful after that.

While in Oklahoma, one of my fellow student's brothers flew down in a P-47 Thunderbolt fighter before leaving for combat in Europe. He gave us an air show that was one for the books, buzzing the flight line with a dazzling array of maneuvers while we stood watching with mouths agape. He did rolls, flew upside down, flew straight up and then down toward the deck in a power dive, and so on. It was the most thrilling ten minutes of my entire naval career and reinforced my desire to be a pilot some day.

After mechanics training, we spent two weeks learning about radar, and then we transferred to Mayport, Florida, to gunnery school to learn how to shoot. It was about this time that that the United States dropped the atomic bombs at Hiroshima and Nagasaki, Japan, which brought an end to World War II. That was a real cause for celebration among the guys in our unit, particularly since it meant we wouldn't have to face the dangers of combat. I was glad along with everyone else, but I also felt that maybe I was missing out on something, too.

After that, it was a little odd to still be in training, without much chance of ever seeing combat. Some of the men decided to stay and make a career out of the Navy, and they got promoted and moved to a permanent assignment as aircraft mechanics. Most of us decided there wasn't going to be a lot of opportunity in a peacetime Navy, so we decided to wait out the balance of our enlistment. We were given more menial assignments that were suited to our rank of Seaman First Class. I was assigned to pilot a "Liberty Launch," which is a fifty-five-foot boat that goes from a mainland dock to an aircraft carrier moored out in the harbor. In essence, I was a shuttle driver, transporting sailors back and forth from ship to shore as needed. Not much of a job really.

Since the Navy had far more enlisted personnel than it needed in peacetime, I took advantage of an early release program that ended my enlistment in March 1946. After receiving the "Ruptured Duckling" separation patch in San Francisco, I traveled to the small farming community of Kuna in southwest Idaho, where my parents had moved while I was in the Navy. I'd been pretty lonesome for home while in training, so I was glad to be with my family again even though it was strange not to go home to Clearfield where all my friends were. It was even stranger to find myself a civilian again, left to wonder what I ought to do with my life. Still, with the postwar economy running along at full tilt, the future looked pretty bright.

CHAPTER TWO

TOW-REEL OPERATOR TO AIR FORCE PILOT

After working at a few odd jobs, I enrolled at Boise State Junior College in 1947. I still wasn't clear what I wanted to do for a living, but I continued to have a fascination with airplanes. I thought about finding an opportunity to do some flying on a regular basis. After exploring a number of options, I joined the Idaho Air National Guard in Boise as a tow-reel operator. My unit had a couple of B-26 bombers that were used to tow targets for the P-51 Mustang fighter pilots to practice their shooting. My job was to ride in the back of the B-26 and release a bundle of netting that contained a large red or white banner approximately thirty feet long by five feet deep. The banner was tethered to our aircraft by a one-eighth-inch steel cable wound around a one-and-a-half-foot reel that I controlled (the mechanism looked something like a giant fishing reel). The top edge of the banner had a large metal pipe attached to it, while the bottom edge was secured to a lead weight to give it stability in the wind. At the appointed time, I threw the bundle out through a hole in the bottom of the airplane, and when the wind caught it, the reel would take off like a fishing line snagged by a barracuda. I'd have to apply a brake to slow it down so the cable wouldn't snap when it reached maximum extension. The brake required a lot of pressure and almost glowed red-hot from the friction. I would notify my pilot when the banner was trailing at about 1,200 feet, and he would pass the word to the Mustang pilots who had followed us out to the firing range that they were now clear to make "hot" passes at the banner with their .50-caliber machine guns. When the live-fire exercises were over, my crew and I would drop altitude and release the banner to the ground for the fighter pilots to be scored on their competency. It was hard but exciting work, and it gave me a chance to get airborne fairly regularly.

I also decided to get active in our local church activities, which took me to the church farm one day to work on a sugar-beet project. At the end of the day, there was an ice-cream social around a bonfire to help everyone relax. It was there that I spied a beautiful young woman named Realla Johnson, the sister of a friend of mine, and I was smitten immediately. In the conversation that followed, I found her to be an extremely intelligent person who was in her final semester of a nursing program.

I was determined to ask her out on a date, so I went to the dormitory where she lived to try to strike up a conversation. I was really nervous, and when the "dorm mother" who supervised the girls in the dormitory answered the door, I was so unnerved that I actually forgot Realla's name when she asked who I wanted to see. It was embarrassing, just stammering like that, and she told me to "beat it" while closing the door in my face. I was walking down the street dejectedly when Realla's name came back into my mind, so I turned around and marched back to get past the warden. Realla seemed happy to see me, and that initiated our courtship. About a year later, I proposed to her during Thanksgiving break in 1947, and I was so happy when she smiled and said yes.

We were married in the Salt Lake Temple on St. Patrick's Day, March 17, 1948. Ezra Taft Benson, an apostle in our church, agreed to perform the wedding ceremony. He'd been one of our local church leaders in Boise, and even though he was extremely busy in his church assignment, he excused himself from other meetings to be with us. It made for a terrific day and the perfect start to the more than fifty-five years we've been together.

After a short honeymoon to California in a borrowed car, we returned to Boise, where I continued going to school. Perhaps because of Realla's work in medicine, I started taking pre-med classes at Boise State, but I soon learned that I had absolutely no aptitude for it. In fact, one day my zoology professor asked me to stay after class. He told me that I had no chance of passing the class and that it would be a real mistake for me to stay in pre-med. When I expressed some resistance, telling him I really wanted to be a doctor, he made me an offer. "Fisher, I'll tell you what I'll do. If you drop out of the class, I'll give you an A. If you stay in the class, you'll get an F—your choice."

"I'll take the A."

Thus ended my medical career. It was a good decision, since I was spending long hours studying to pass tests that other students with natural ability could get A's on with very little effort.

Shortly after that, I transferred from Boise State Junior College to the University of Utah in Salt Lake City. By this time, I was seriously contemplating a military career. To enjoy the kind of lifestyle we desired, I'd need to become a commissioned officer, since the income and quality of housing enjoyed by officers far outweigh that received by the enlisted ranks. I also wanted to be a pilot, which narrowed the list to the Navy and the newly formed Air Force (which had become a separate military branch rather than a division of the Army shortly after World War II). The Air Force seemed to offer the best chance at having something of a traditional family life. (In the Navy, officers often had to spend six or more months at sea.) I figured the best way to join was to enroll in the Air Force Reserve Officers Training Corps (ROTC) while I finished my studies. The Idaho Air National Guard consented to let me transfer to the Utah Air National Guard, where I continued to work as a tow-reel operator.

I looked forward to registering at the University of Utah. In those days, students registered for classes by waiting in line for permission to go into the gymnasium to collect IBM punch cards for the classes they desired. Classes were allocated on a first-come, first-serve basis, and as a new transfer student I was placed toward the back of the line. By the time

I got to the Air Force ROTC table, I was given the unhappy news that the class was full. I tried to talk them into making an exception, but to no avail.

A couple of weeks before the first quarter ended, I asked the colonel in charge of the program if there was any chance of getting into the course, thinking that perhaps somebody had washed out or dropped.

"You really want to get in, don't you?"

"I think this is what I want to do with my life."

"Well, why don't you go ahead and attend ROTC classes from now until the end of the quarter, and if you pass the final examination, we'll give you credit for the quarter and formally enroll you in the program."

I burst into a grin and said, "Yes, sir!" Unlike the zoology class, this course work came naturally, and I easily passed the examination. That's how my Air Force career got started.

Once accepted into ROTC, I focused on getting accepted to flight school. The competition was fierce, with only six or seven cadets chosen out of 200 applicants.

The first obstacle was passing both the Officer Qualifying exam and the Flight Aptitude Test. I studied relentlessly and passed these two written tests. Next, I went to Hamilton Field, near San Francisco, for rigorous physical testing. It was here that most cadets washed out of the program. One of the most challenging tests was the centrifuge, in which they strap you into a device like a dentist's chair and spin you around while you move your head from side to side. Periodically they'd stop the chair and order you to point in a specified direction, such as north. If you failed to point in the correct direction, you washed out. That was just one of a whole battery of tests that were used to test our coordination, dexterity, and ability to respond quickly in adverse conditions. I passed all elements of the exams and was cleared for flight school.

When I reported to Marana Air Force Base in Arizona a few months later on January 10, 1953, it was with the knowledge that the Air Force prided itself on a 50-percent attrition rate in each phase of the upcoming school. The first six weeks were spent in ground school, learning the principles of flight and the mechanical systems on an airplane. We then trained on a propeller-driven AT-6 Texan aircraft. I'll never forget my first solo flight. My assigned instructor spent a few hours observing me flying touch-and-go patterns, then allowed me to land the aircraft by myself. Tapping me on the on the shoulder, he asked, "Do you think you can fly by yourself?"

"You bet!" I shot back confidently, although I wasn't nearly so sure on the inside.

"Okay, let me get out and you take it up."

With that, he strapped his parachute into the backseat and crawled out of the Texan. "Take it up, shoot three touch-and-go's, and then bring it back down."

I was scared but also thrilled. This was the moment I'd been waiting for. I made a good, clean takeoff and circled out high over the airfield, just as I'd done on the earlier flight. I slowly banked the aircraft into an approach toward the runway and lowered the flaps to slow my airspeed to begin my descent. The airplane responded beautifully, and I executed a perfect approach to the runway. Just when the wheels touched the ground, I pushed the throttle ahead for full acceleration, and the aircraft leaped off the ground like an eager steeplechase horse launching into a jump. Before I knew it, I was back up in the air, circling the airfield and preparing for the second approach. Everything went just as planned—every bit as good as when my instructor was with me. On the third approach, I let the aircraft settle in for a good solid landing. I could hardly suppress a grin as I taxied off the runway and onto the tarmac, where I shut the engine down at the preassigned spot. I went over and saluted my instructor, who said, "Congratulations, Fisher, you're a solo pilot!"

Believe me, nothing in the world could have sounded quite as good to my ears. I'd made it past one of the major hurdles of flight school.

Unfortunately, I didn't do quite so well a few weeks later on my check ride. After forty hours of solo flight, each pilot has to be "checked out" by an Air Force officer not connected to the flight school. This is a standard procedure the Air Force uses to determine if a pilot has met all requirements to operate a specific aircraft proficiently and safely. As luck would have it, a cocky young lieutenant was assigned to be my rater, and his condescending attitude rattled me. We took off, and I did everything just fine until he pulled the throttle back to "idle" and told me to make a forced landing. I did everything the way I was supposed to, maintaining the aircraft in flight as we descended without power for a proper landing but, in the anxiety of the moment, I forgot to put the landing gear down. It was a stupid mistake, because an alarm even sounds in your headset to remind you to get the wheels down. It sounded loud and clear, but it was too late for me to pass the test. The lieutenant leaned forward and said, “Take it around and let’s go home.” I was frustrated with myself and knew I hadn’t passed.

When we were back on the ground, he said that he’d talk with my instructor and have him ride with me a few more times until I got it right. That was humiliating. After that many hours of solo flying, it was something of a disgrace to have your instructor go back up with you. Nonetheless, I was relieved that I had been given another chance. My own instructor wasn’t all that concerned and just took me up a couple of times to practice the procedure before scheduling a follow-up check ride. The same rater climbed into the aircraft, and as we gained altitude I prepared myself mentally for whatever he chose to throw at me. I made a precise 90-degree turn and waited for instructions. He pulled the throttle back to idle and simply said, “Forced landing.” I wasn’t going to make the same mistake twice. Concentrating on the procedure, I successfully banked the aircraft into a turn that brought us into position with the field and then followed each step of the protocol with precision. When I reached the point where I was supposed to drop the landing gear, I pushed the lever firmly and listened for the wheels to lock into position. As soon as the landing gear locked, the lieutenant said curtly, “That’s good enough for me. Let’s go home.”

I breathed a huge sigh of relief—particularly when I learned that my overall scores easily placed me in the top half of the class. Out of the four cadets assigned to my instructor, I was the only one to make it.

At this point in my career, I had to make a decision about

what type of aircraft I wanted to fly. One of my favorite instructors at the school was a man named Carl Anderson, who had been a B-17 bomber pilot in World War II. He loved the large aircraft and naturally steered his students toward bombers. I went along with the crowd, which really pleased Carl. Just before completing the necessary paperwork, however, the Air Force sent a couple of jet fighters down from Williams Air Force Base. These fighter pilots gave us the most astonishing twenty-minute air show I'd ever seen. They did eight-point rolls, chandelles, and lazy eights, all of which left me breathless. After this spectacular show, I went directly from the airfield to Carl Anderson's office. "Carl, I've changed my mind—I want to go with the fighters!"

He was disappointed but said that I was probably right, and he'd strike the orders accordingly. I was almost too excited to talk. The thought of flying a fighter was everything I could ever have hoped for, and now it was about to become a reality.

Shortly thereafter, we packed the car, and I took my wife and two boys to Williams Air Force Base in central Arizona to enroll in Fighter School.

After about six weeks of ground training, I got to take my first flight in a T-33 (the two-seat version of the F-80 jet fighter). The acceleration of a jet aircraft is really something—much smoother than a propeller-driven aircraft, yet quieter and more powerful. It also has a very different feeling as the engine comes up to speed. The propeller-driven aircraft can wind up to maximum RPM almost instantly, while a jet engine slowly increases the speed of its turbines until they reach a certain critical point; then it accelerates rapidly.

Probably the most notable difference in flying a jet aircraft is the amount of G-force the pilot is subjected to because of high velocity. Most pilots are capable of pulling about nine G's of force, when properly suited. A G is equivalent to one gravitational pull on your body, so just standing or sitting is one G. Put another way, if you normally weigh 200 pounds at one G, you would experience what it's like to weigh 400 pounds at two G's, 600 pounds at three G's, and so on. At around five G's a pilot may experience a condition called "gun-barrel vision," where blood is forced away from the brain, making him lose his peripheral vision. He may also develop double vision. If he pulls in a little bit tighter, increasing the G-force, he might go into what's called a "gray-out," where he loses visibility all together and can't see anything. Any tighter and he's likely to lose consciousness.[1] I experienced a blackout just once, while flying as an observer, and when I came to, my body was convulsing from the experience. It was very frightening.

To counter the effect of G-forces, a fighter pilot wears a "G-suit," which consists of a girdle and series of bladders around the legs and stomach that automatically inflate and deflate with G-force pressure. Under G-forces, these bladders tighten up to keep blood from pooling in the extremities.

---

1. A pilot can also initiate a dive that leads to a "red out," in which blood is forced to the brain, causing a loss of consciousness. Unfortunately, there's no way to protect against a "red out" other than to avoid making the maneuvers that would cause it.

A few months into flight school, shortly after I certified to fly solo on the F-80, I contracted a disease called valley fever that is unique to the San Joaquin Valley and the area where Williams is located. It's almost identical to tuberculosis but not contagious. I discovered the problem during a cross-country flight with my instructor out to the West Coast and back. When we landed at Williams, my lungs and back hurt so bad that I needed help getting out of the aircraft—it came on that suddenly. The doctors took me directly to the hospital and said I'd probably need to stay there for at least a week since I'd developed a spot on my lung that needed immediate treatment with antibiotics. I was actually in there for thirty days. It was really discouraging, since the men I'd been going through school with got to "check out" on the F-80 while I was lying on my back in bed. The guys were good enough to come to the hospital and give me "play-by-plays" of what it was like, which I appreciated, but I felt so bad being out of the action.

When I finally healed, the Air Force stood by me and simply washed me back one class. I started out in class 1953-A but wound up in 1953-B instead. Fortunately, I took up right where I left off, and the flying wasn't any different than the class I'd been in before.

Part of the final test for fighter school was an instrument check, where you fly the aircraft with a hood over your head so you can't see out the forward canopy. The test includes a complicated series of maneuvers: takeoff and landing, formation flying, and certain types of aerobatics that simulate an air-to-air engagement. At one point in the test, the two wingmen break off and attempt to establish a radar-lock on your position. If a pilot lets somebody get a successful lock, he gets a pink slip, which means a failing ride. We could only get so many pink slips before they washed us out of the school. It was pretty unnerving to fly with the hood, but it was essential to learn how to operate the aircraft in all conditions, including adverse weather, night flying, and high-speed combat.

As the day for my final flight check approached, my wife thought I was losing my mind. I was simply obsessed with being in the top 50 percent of the class so I could graduate and go full-time. I'd go to sleep at night memorizing procedures and practicing drills over and over in my mind. Sometimes I'd talk to myself, repeating each step in the sequence. Before the school was complete, I could literally do it in my sleep, since I'd fallen asleep so many nights rehearsing.

To ease the pressure, Realla and I sometimes went golfing in the evenings, which was a pleasant diversion in the winter days in Arizona. I loved playing with our little boys, as well.

The final requirement for the year's training at the flight and fighter schools was to plan and execute a cross-country trip, including planned stops for fuel along the way. There's a lot of math and navigation involved. My trip was successful, and I passed both courses well within the acceptable range for a full-time commission.

Graduation was one of the greatest events of my life, because it meant I now had a career that would support our family while allowing me to fly the aircraft I had come to love. The next steps in my training were instrumentation school at Moody Air Force base in Georgia, followed by gunnery training at Tyndall Air Force Base in Panama City, Florida.

Unlike primary training in Arizona, these schools were designed to test our skills in varying flight conditions, particularly adverse weather and night flying. The course at Moody was six weeks long, with intense study and practice. There was an incident here that I'll never forget because of its tragic ending. We had about twenty pilots who went through the school with me, and we were in the air as often as possible. Even though our instructors were always on the lookout for difficult weather patterns so we could have experience in flying through a thunderhead, the storms were particularly violent that year with crosscurrents, wind shears, and turbulence, to the point that it was too rough to go up on a lot of days. We were falling behind schedule. Perhaps because of that, the decision was made to take us up one day, even though the weather officer predicted some nasty thunderstorms. We were pressing our luck a bit, but it looked like we'd have a window of opportunity to get up and down during an expected lull in the storm, so they put up about twenty airplanes. We were flying T-33 jet fighters, and everyone was flying in and out of some of the rougher weather, just to get used to handling the aircraft in those types of conditions. When word was received that the main thunderhead was moving in the direction of the base, the flight controllers ordered us to burn our tip tanks (fuel tanks on the end of each wing) and then return to the base as soon as possible.

The storm moved much faster than expected, so ground

control ordered us to make an approach even if we hadn't had time to burn off the fuel in the tips. With the urgency of the weather pressing us, everybody headed to the initial approach, with those at the front of the pack slowing down to perhaps 125 miles per hour to get into the pattern. I was going about 250 miles per hour, so I had to break out and circle around to reenter the pattern a second time. One of the guys in the front of the pack was getting ready to land and pitched out[2] for a proper approach just as a lightning bolt cracked directly in his flight path. The strike must have blinded him, because he rolled over too fast and too far and crashed on the runway. The ensuing fireball made it obvious that he'd been killed in the crash. That raised the anxiety level even further for those of us left in the flight pattern.

Beyond the horror of his crash, we now had a new problem. With nineteen aircraft still in the air, there was no way we could land at Moody until they'd had a chance to clear the debris from the crash. With the weather growing ever more ominous, ground control quickly reassigned us to

---

2. "Pitch out" refers to a landing pattern in which a group of aircraft approach the air base in single file on a flight path that is parallel to the runway. As the lead aircraft reaches the end of the runway at 800 feet altitude, he pitches out (pushes the control stick to the left while pulling it back toward his body to keep the aircraft level) to initiate a descending 360-degree turn that will bring him directly in line with the runway at the end of the turn so he can land. The aircraft directly behind him starts counting to three after the lead aircraft pitches out, then initiates his own pitch-out and roll to land behind him. This sequence is repeated until all aircraft are safely on the ground. It's the best way to sequence the landing. In this case, the pattern was too crowded, so I had to turn in the opposite direction of the pitch-out and circle back around at 800 feet to get in line for a second attempt.

other airbases in the area. My primary landing field was Tyndall Air Force Base in Florida, which was approximately 100 miles away, with an alternate at Dale Mabry Air Force Base near Tallahassee. I'd never been to Tyndall Air Force Base and had no idea where it was, so there I was in the dark with a thunderstorm crackling all around my aircraft, hurriedly pulling out my flashlight and map to find Tyndall Air Force Base. I found my location at Moody and calculated the flight path to Tyndall Air Force Base.

I was still new at this, so I calculated in my mind that if I gained a lot of altitude I could coast into one of the fields if I ran low on fuel. The T-33 is a very forgiving aircraft with a terrific glide ratio. At 40,000 feet it would glide nearly 100 miles with a dead engine. So I climbed to 40,000 feet and headed for Dale Mabry Air Force Base. Once I made it there safely, I found that I was right on target for Tyndall Air Force Base with enough fuel left, so I kept on course for the primary field. Even though I'd never been there, I was confident I could find it. Maybe I was over-confident, because when I got to where the base should have been, I couldn't see anything on the ground that resembled an airfield. It was awfully frightening for an inexperienced student flying in the dark in severe weather and totally out of sight from the ground (40,000 feet is approximately eight miles up). In as level a voice as I could muster, I called the approach control that was vectoring us in and told him I couldn't see the field. He replied that they were turning on the Selingometer, which is a light that pulses into the clouds so a pilot can spot it from the air. He assured me that it was flashing, but I still couldn't see it. I told him in a breathless voice that I was pretty sure of my navigation but I couldn't see the field. At that point he asked me, "How high are you?"

"I'm at 40,000 feet!"

He laughed as he said, "Well, come on down so you can see the ground!"

I was so high in the air that I couldn't see through the natural haze caused by the humidity near the ocean. A little embarrassed, I descended to 20,000 feet, which brought me below the haze, and it was just a beautiful night. Sure enough, there were the lights of Tyndall Air Force Base blazing brightly for the entire world to see. I made my assigned approach and successfully landed the aircraft.

Seeing the effects of the crash from the night before left an eerie feeling in my stomach when I returned to Moody the next day, knowing that a man I'd worked and flown with had perished.

Once we successfully completed instrument school, we were assigned to move to Tyndall for the next phase of our training. I wanted Realla and the boys to join me for this part of our training. After I had completed my training in Arizona, she had moved back to Kuna to stay with her parents while I was off to Georgia for six weeks, but gunnery school would last long enough that we could rent temporary housing and be together again. Probably the easiest thing would have been for her to fly straight to Tyndall, but we wanted some adventure and a new car, so I thought of a way to do both. First, I ordered a brand-new Buick Special station wagon and indicated we'd pick it up at the factory in Flint, Michigan. Second, I asked Realla to drop off our old car in Nampa, Idaho, and catch a train for Chicago, where I'd meet her and the boys for a drive down to Panama City. The plan was that I'd use the first day of my four-day leave to get to Flint, pick up the car, and then drive to Chicago to meet her on Saturday. Unfortunately, plans don't always work out the way they're supposed to. I didn't get out of Moody on time, and I was running late. The bus schedule that was supposed to get me north got messed up somehow, so I finally decided to take my chances hitchhiking. A fellow picked me up in a huge sixteen-wheel rig, and when I told him I'd driven for Consolidated Freightways after the war, he asked if I'd like to take a turn behind the wheel. I told him yes, because I thought maybe I could make up some lost time. So he slept while I drove his truck down the Pennsylvania Turnpike. I'm afraid I took advantage of that great road to really put some miles under the wheels in a short time, but it still wasn't fast enough to get me where I needed to go on time. So I got off in a little town near the bus depot and caught a bus for Chicago. By now I was getting pretty desperate, because I could just see my family waiting at the train station with no one to meet them. I said a little prayer, and the thought came to me to call the terminal manager at the train station in Chicago. I actually got through, and when I explained my problem and told him I was in the Air Force, he told me to relax because he'd take care of everything. He met my wife and the boys (and our dog) and took them to a hotel, checked them in, arranged for dinner, then called me back and told me that everything was okay. I was so grateful and relieved. He acted like it was nothing and told me he was glad to help one of the men in uniform. That really struck me as significant. His kindness taught me how much people appreciate those who serve in the Armed Forces, and it reinforced the sense of pride I felt in being in the Air Force.

I arrived in Flint later that night, picked up the car the next morning, and made a direct beeline for Chicago, where I found my family happy and anxious to see me. We spent the afternoon together in Chicago, touring the area just a bit, and then headed off for Panama City the next day.

One of the reasons I had been so anxious was that Realla was eight months pregnant with our third child, and I was worried about her going into labor. We plotted all the hospitals along the way in case she started into labor, but she didn't, and we had a wonderful drive together through Tennessee and the other southern states. Our third son, Robbin, was born about three weeks after we arrived in Florida.

After getting Realla and the boys settled into temporary housing, I began weapons training. A jet aircraft has three types of armaments—machine guns, bombs, and rockets. At Tyndall Air Force Base, we trained on firing the .50-caliber machine guns and dropping bombs. Machine guns are used for two activities—strafing the enemy to provide support to ground troops and fighting air-to-air combat with enemy aircraft. While there is some chance of actually hitting an enemy and causing damage during aerial combat, the more likely outcome of firing the machine guns is that you'll force him to waver from his attack path so he can't secure a good fix on you to shoot you down. Because the machine guns fire in a fixed direction, you actually maneuver the aircraft to properly sight on your target.

There's a lot to think about in an air combat situation—

flying the aircraft to maintain proper flight, paying attention to both friendly and enemy aircraft in the area, and firing your guns to good effect. At speeds between 300 to 500 miles per hour, everything goes by in a blur to a new pilot. You could be in and out of harm's way before you even realized what had happened.

We also practiced bombing using various colored smoke bombs. The target was a bale of hay in the middle of a large field, with markers extending out in each direction to show the distance from the target. The goal was to hit the center of this "bull's-eye" with unique colored smoke. In a T-33 training aircraft, you approach the target at approximately 250 miles per hour, with bomb racks loaded with little thirty-five-pound smoke bombs. As you reach the "Initial Point of Contact," you look through a scope positioned directly in front of the pilot on the instrument panel. The scope has a lighted grid superimposed on the lens that displays the bomb sight. Since the target is identified in advance of the flight, you have to pre-program the scope for the best approach to that particular target. For example, you might plan a 45-degree descent from a predetermined altitude at 250 miles per hour. With that information in the targeting computer, the scope shows your progress as you approach the point where you should release the bombs. Once you reach the spot where the lines converge, it's time to press the release button on the control stick. Because of the aircraft's forward speed, the bombs follow an arc down to the ground that hopefully ends right at the bale of hay. It took a lot of practice before I could hit anywhere near the center of the target area.

On successful completion of gunnery school, I was cleared for active duty in Air Defense Command, the front-line defense for the American homeland. I'd made it! We began preparing to transfer to a permanent posting.

CHAPTER THREE

ON ALERT IN CHICAGO

THE AIR FORCE GAVE ME A choice of two assignments. Realla and I talked and decided that we'd like to go to Chicago. Having grown up in relatively rural areas, we decided to try living in the excitement and activity of a large urban area. The Air Force made arrangements to transfer our household goods while we drove up in our station wagon with the boys. Upon arriving, we found that housing was pretty tight, so we moved into a motel temporarily.

I reported to Base Command at the 42nd Fighter Interceptor Squadron at O'Hare Air Force Base, where my flight commander welcomed us and made arrangements for me to attend ground school to train for certification on the F-86D aircraft that I'd be flying as part of Air Defense Command. Each time a pilot is assigned to fly an unfamiliar aircraft, he needs to be trained and checked out before standing on active alert. So it was back to the classroom to learn the details of this new airplane and then into a sophisticated flight simulator.

There is no training version of the F-86 because it has a single seat, which means you fly solo from your very first flight. The flight commander stands on the wing while you get in the cockpit and orient yourself to the controls, then observes as you fire up the engine. If everything looks okay, he dismounts from your aircraft and gets into his own F-86D to shadow you during takeoff and flight, just in case there is any trouble. The F-86D carries twenty-four small rockets in the belly of the airplane, and since our squadron was called to stand on active alert, we had to practice to fire the rockets safely. Of course, we couldn't shoot the practice rockets anywhere near Chicago because it's too densely populated, so we'd fly to a remote location in Arizona to practice on an open range. One of the pilots in our squadron proved that point one day quite by accident. The rockets are loaded into a pod suspended from the bottom of the aircraft. When he stepped on the ladder to mount to the cockpit, the static electricity in his shoes somehow triggered the rockets, and they streaked off at ground level, totally out of control. They flew parallel to the ground for nearly two miles before exploding in a private girl's academy next to the base. Fortunately, it was nighttime and there were no people in the buildings, but the Air Force was in trouble with civilian authorities for that one.

After approximately ten training flights, including rocket practice in Arizona, the flight commander certified me as "combat ready," which allowed me to take my place in the regular rotation. After all the long months of training, I was finally an active Air Force pilot. That was a good day and a cause for celebration at the Fisher household, which was still living in a hotel at that point.

Here's what a typical training cycle was like for fighter pilots assigned to Air Defense Command:

• *Day 1—training.* We arrived at the flight line by 08:00 in the morning. After a briefing to receive any special instructions and learn where the practice missions would be for the day, we reported at the flight line at approximately 10:00 for the first mission. A second mission followed lunch, ending at approximately 16:00 to provide time to secure the aircraft and other gear. On these training missions, we'd fly intercepts against each other, practice simulated shooting at targets, and experiment with various escape maneuvers in case one of us got into some kind of trouble. These were the days that kept our skills fresh and up to standard. We dismissed at 17:00 to return home to have dinner and enjoy the evening with our families.

• *Day 2—stand alert.* We arrived at a special alert hangar by 08:00. At O'Hare Air Force Base we had four small hangars at the end of each of the military runways that housed a separate "alert aircraft," fully loaded with rockets. The pilots on alert spent the day studying their procedure manuals and other assignments but always with flight gear on, ready to go at a moment's notice. A radar installation near the base tracked everything in the area for a 200-mile radius, monitoring all the commercial, military, and civilian aircraft flying in and out of the area. All these aircraft had to be identified. If an unidentified aircraft entered the airspace, the radar controllers had a limited amount of time to try to establish contact. If they couldn't verify a proper authentication within the prescribed time, the radar controller pushed a red button in the center of his console that sounded a large horn in the alert hangars. That horn was the signal to "scramble." From the moment the horn blared, we had just five minutes to race to our aircraft, fire up the engines, and taxi onto the runway into proper position for takeoff to run an intercept. If the unidentified aircraft was still considered potentially hostile, the Civilian Air Control Tower provided the initial coordinates for the flight path needed to bring us under military control along with clearance for immediate takeoff. After just a few minutes in the air, authority was transferred to a military controller, who provided appropriate vectors to bring us into contact with the intruder. We flew at maximum speed to the errant aircraft and pulled up on each of its wings in order to determine the nature of the aircraft and its mission. Since we were flying in peacetime during those early years of the 1950s, we never encountered an actual military threat. More often it was some kind of civilian or commercial aircraft that had simply forgotten to check in or perhaps had lost its radio. It was always interesting to see the look on a pilot's face when two F-86 fighters pulled into position on each wing. He'd move pretty fast to get in touch with us.

• *Day 3—off duty.* On the third day, we had time off to stay home with the family, catch up on assignments, or do whatever we liked. It was the reward for enduring the tension and tedium of standing on alert the previous day.

Then, the next day the cycle started over again.

The three-day cycle kept our skills at their highest while we stayed alert for any threat to the airways. I liked it because it meant I had a lot of time to spend with my family, as well as plenty of time in the air working to perfect my skills in handling the aircraft.

Housing was a real problem. The motel we were staying in was relatively inexpensive but still more expensive than renting an apartment or buying a house. So on the off-duty day in the rotation, I often went out looking for bigger and better accommodations. One day, I saw a man working on a small building with four apartments. I stopped and asked if he'd be interested in renting it, but he said he wasn't ready to have anyone move in. I explained how desperate our situation was, and he finally relented, saying that he had some carpentry work to finish but that we could move into one of the apartments in a couple of weeks. Rather than absorb the cost of staying in the motel for another two weeks, I requested a brief leave of absence and took the family on a short vacation to Idaho to visit our parents and family. When we returned, the apartment was ready, and we moved in. It had a yard where the boys could play, and it gave us a chance to settle into a permanent civilian ward at church.[1] In no time, we were fully involved in our ward and happy to be part of the community. I was asked to serve as elders quorum president, and Realla was called to serve as Relief Society president,[2]

---

1. A ward is a local congregation in The Church of Jesus Christ of Latter-day Saints (LDS).

2. The elders quorum and Relief Society are the men's and women's service auxiliaries for lay members of The Church of Jesus Christ of Latter-day Saints.

giving her the chance to get to know all the women. We came to love the people in the ward, particularly since there's an unusually close feeling among the members when you live in an area where the LDS Church is in the minority.

We also enjoyed playing golf together in the summer and going into the city of Chicago once in a while to see a show or enjoy the shopping. We took the boys down to the Navy Pier on Lake Michigan, which is an amusement park with Ferris wheels and other rides, and we enjoyed the zoo and other activities available in that large metropolitan area.

After more than a year on active duty, I started feeling pretty comfortable with the routine of flying alerts and actually gained enough confidence to cause some trouble one day by playing a joke during a practice alert. In order to test the reliability of the Air Defense Command, the base periodically scheduled an aircraft to enter our airspace with instructions to the local ground control to display it as an unidentified intruder. Both the civilian and military controllers knew it was a test, but the pilots weren't informed until they reached the point of intercept.

On this particular day, they scrambled us, and we took off well within our five-minute window, accelerating with afterburners at maximum thrust to the vectors assigned by our civilian and military controllers. As we moved within radar range of the unidentified aircraft, we were supposed to report, "I've got a Judy," which meant the pilot would take the intercept from that point forward. It's also at that point that the controllers were supposed to tell us that this was a test, with instructions to break off the engagement.

In this incident, the unidentified airplane was flying

down Lake Michigan at a high rate of speed when I came within range and called out that I had a Judy. Even though I was confident that this was just a test, in just a moment or two I successfully locked onto him with radar and had him in my scope. When there was no immediate response from the base, I decided to shake things up a little, so I said into my microphone, "I'm taking a Judy and understand that I'm clear to fire!"

You never heard such a racket in your life. The radio silence was shattered as the pilot of the airplane shouted frantically not to shoot while the ground controller was telling me not to fire. There was so much radio traffic that everyone started blocking each other out. Well, I knew who it was, and I never had any intention of firing, but they didn't know that. I confirmed their "do not shoot" order and returned to base. Once we landed, our officers called a briefing and told us in no uncertain terms never to do that again, to which I replied, "You're supposed to clear the Judy and tell us it's a fictitious target, not a real one. We have to assume it's the real thing if you don't tell us otherwise." The ground controllers were a lot more responsive after that.

It was several months later that I experienced an unfortunate flying incident, one that could have been fatal. Our group commander needed some flying time to maintain his certification, so he asked my flight commander to go along as his instructor and organize a mission. My flight commander chose me to fly wing, accompanied by a young second lieutenant, the newest pilot on the team, as my student. We filed a flight plan to Tyndall Air Force Base in Florida flying T-33s, with my student and me in the lead on the outbound leg of the journey. On the way out, the colonel flew the formation on me, sliding in and out to make the join-ups and other maneuvers that were required for his recertification. He was kind of shaky but did well enough to qualify. We made a good solid landing at Tyndall Air Force Base, and in recognition of the colonel's rank, a blue staff car came out to take us to the base PX to buy an ice-cream cone while the local ground crew refueled our aircraft. The weather officer told us to expect some poor weather on the way back to Chicago.

We took off fine and climbed to 38,000 feet for the two-hour trip back, with the colonel in the lead. As we approached Chicago, the tower told us the weather was down, with marginal landing conditions at best. We conferred over the radio and decided the best thing to do was go ahead and land as soon as possible, before the weather deteriorated any further. The colonel made a banking turn and penetrated the clouds to make the approach. Unfortunately, he turned early and came in too high above the runway. We pulled up and out of the clouds. I was right next to him, as I was supposed to be, and he indicated visually that he was having trouble with his radio. He signaled that we should do a fly-around, with me assuming the lead for the landing. I wasn't expecting to take the lead, so I scrambled to find the appropriate map, then rolled out and went ahead of him to find the proper approach to start down on the penetration. As we descended into the clouds, it was pitch-black outside the canopy, and the weather was actually below minimum, even though the tower hadn't informed us of that. Sometimes they fudged a bit on the weather conditions so commercial freightliners could continue to land.

I turned up the lights in the cockpit as bright as possible so the colonel could see me, and I signaled for him to lower his landing gear by pointing my thumb down. I thought he was looking right at me, but apparently he wasn't, because he was unprepared when I dropped my gear. When the wheels descend, an immediate drag is created on the aircraft, which quickly slows your airspeed. The colonel was flying directly beside me, and when I lost airspeed he was still moving at regular speed. By the time he saw what was happening he pulled up, but too late to avoid hitting my wing and drilling a hole in my fuel tank on the end of the wing. I'll never forget looking out the canopy and seeing nothing but the belly of his airplane directly up against my starboard side as he banked hard in an attempt to recover from the collision. The contact had also torn a hole in his fuel tank, and I thought for sure he was going to crash. I fought to stabilize my own aircraft and did my best to maintain a level flight pattern, hoping he'd recover and follow me in. Fortunately, the instructor pilot in the backseat of the colonel's aircraft was an excellent pilot, and he grabbed control of the aircraft and brought it right back into formation after the collision. In another second or two, the lights of the runway came into view, and we set our airplanes down safely on the runway with the instructor holding a tight pattern on my left wing.

As soon as we were safe on the deck, we taxied to a hangar, where the maintenance people were waiting for us. As soon as the colonel got out of his plane, he came striding over to our aircraft with a solemn look on his face. I braced myself but was relieved to hear him say, "Bernie, we won't write this one up."

"That's all right with me, sir—you're the boss!"

Then he went over and raised heck with the people in the weather center for leaving the field open when it should have been closed. I was so relieved I could hardly believe it. It certainly gave my student some real-world experience in a hurry. The collision reminded me that the difference between life and death is sometimes measured in inches, and I felt that our family prayers for my safety had been answered that day.

The days and weeks fed into each other, and as our family approached the three-year mark in my service, we had settled into a comfortable and enjoyable routine. So it wasn't exactly the best news when I got a call indicating that it was time to rotate to Chitose, Japan, on the north island of Hokkaido. Although we knew we couldn't stay in Chicago forever, Realla was sad to leave her friends and pack everything up again for another transfer. It was worse when we learned that the housing situation in Japan was so tight it would probably take at least a year before they could help us find family housing. We decided that Realla would go back to Idaho to live near her family while I went solo to Japan. That's sometimes the downside of military life, since you can't really turn down a transfer—particularly as a young first lieutenant.

CHAPTER FOUR

JAPAN AT THE BEGINNING OF THE COLD WAR

AFTER HELPING THE FAMILY relocate to Idaho, I flew to Japan by commercial airliner and took up residence at the 4th TAC Fighter Wing, assigned to the 339th Fighter Interceptor Squadron in Chitose. It was early in the 1950s, and our location placed us approximately 500 miles north of Tokyo and 200 miles east of the Russian coast on the Sea of Japan. In this location, we were part of the first line of defense against Russian sorties out of Vladivostok, 450 miles to the southeast.

Mine was one of four squadrons assigned to the northern area. After getting my bearings at the base, I began the process of having Realla and the boys join me. Base housing was definitely out of the question for at least a year, but I was told that if I could find suitable housing in the town of Chitose, I might be able to move my family's arrival up a few months. Because Japan was economically depressed at the time (it was still less than ten years since World War II), the base insisted that it sign off on all nonbase housing by checking for sanitary conditions, mechanical and electrical safety, and so forth. I found a local realtor to work with, and together we found a tiny, rather homely house that barely met the minimum standard. The realtor told me we could use that to start the paperwork, but by the time Realla and the boys arrived she hoped to find something larger and more comfortable.

The next step was to get the paperwork signed by three different levels of command—my Squadron Command in Chitose, the Division Command at Misawa Air Base, and finally the 5th Air Force in Tokyo. This process sometimes took up to three months. But I missed my family and wanted them with me, so I asked the squadron commander if I could borrow an airplane (which is a lot like a teenager asking his dad if he can borrow the car). He gave his permission, and I enlisted the aid of one of my friends as a copilot. We took off in a T-33 to make each of the required stops. First we got the local signatures. Then we flew to Misawa and finally to 5th Air Force Command. At each step in the process, I'd go to the appropriate officers and ask if they'd sign the papers. They invariably said to leave them and they'd get them back to me, but I insisted that I was hand carrying them and needed their signature on the spot. Most of the officers smiled at my persistence, and everyone signed in the appropriate place. Then I flew back in the reverse order, to show everyone in the chain of command that I had the proper signatures and authority. When I finally made it back to my squadron commander to present him with the final orders, he couldn't believe I'd done it. He told me that when I asked if I could try to move things along, he didn't think there was any chance it would ever happen.

Since we had an infant, permission was granted for me to fly home and assist Realla in the move. On an overseas transfer, the Air Force prefers to store your heavy furniture locally and make temporary furniture available at your destination. Other items are transferred by usual shipping, except for 600 pounds of emergency and current-use items, which can go with you on the trip. We packed accordingly, said our goodbyes to my mother and Realla's parents, and flew to Seattle, Washington, where we boarded a troopship. We could have flown to Japan, but the flight would have been miserable because of the distance and number of refueling stops required in those days of propeller-driven commercial airlines. Travel by boat, on the other hand, was really delightful. Because I was an officer with a wife and three children, we had our own small stateroom and could spend the days enjoying activities on the deck and exploring the ship. In the evening we had dinner with the ship's captain, and the food was superb. On this particular voyage, there were six Air Force pilots bringing their families over, so the boys had other children to play with, and Realla and I had time to get to know the other officers and share stories. There were also some Navy officers and 1,200 Army troops on their way to the Korean War.

On our second or third day out, we encountered some rough weather, and before long more than 1,200 people on board were really sick. I was an officer of the day, responsible for maintaining order in the mess hall, which was pretty easy considering that no one wanted to eat. My family got sick as well, but I was fortunate to experience nothing more than a slightly queasy stomach.

The weather cleared by the time we reached the Hawaiian Islands, and as we passed north of the islands, a flock of albatross flew alongside the boat to keep us company. It was so remarkably beautiful to see the islands floating in the sea as we sat on deck chairs enjoying the tropical sunset.

By the time we arrived in Tokyo, we were all pretty rested and excited to make our way to a new home. We caught a commercial airline flight to Chitose, where we moved into a larger and cleaner home than we had originally listed on our papers. Compared to American homes, however, most Japanese houses were small and drab, including this one, and it was cold and drafty in the winter. It did give us the chance, however, to experience Japanese culture firsthand. We immediately signed up for language lessons so we could communicate more easily with our neighbors. Perhaps because we made the effort to get to know them, the people in the community warmed up to us and treated us really well. They were genuine and caring people. The neighbors used to come over and say, "If you want to go downtown shopping, please let us take care of the children." Our fair-haired boys really stood out in their small community and were a constant source of interest to the Japanese.

Because of the extreme poverty in the northern area, the U.S. military had promised the Japanese government we would employ local civilians for domestic help. When I first arrived in Japan, the four of us who shared a Quonset hut hired a local boy by the name of Charlie. He did the laundry, shined our shoes, and kept our quarters clean. As we started to move out to be with our families, Charlie was left unemployed, placing him in real economic peril. So I hired him to work for us at our house. He was a great help, particularly since he would man the water pump that filled a small reservoir tank on top of the house so gravity could provide us a fresh shower each day. The water was heated by small wood chips that Charlie burned underneath the tank. Realla also hired a maid at a very reasonable price to help with the housework, giving her the chance to get out into the community and go golfing once in a while.

I remember one incident that about broke my heart. I was awakened early one morning by the sound of something rattling our trash cans. There were a lot of rats in Japan, and I worried that they were trying to get into the garbage. When I investigated, however, I discovered it was a person in the process of taking our garbage. I felt bad to see a well-dressed man in white coveralls, with a white hat and white gloves, patiently going through our garbage. He was quickly sorting the garbage into different piles, putting metal items in one can, discarded food for his animals in a second, and cloth that could be reused or sold in a third. Of course, I did nothing to let him know I'd observed his rummaging, as that would be humiliating for him. In the more than three years we spent in Japan, our garbage cans never got full.

I was a lot happier in my job once my family joined me and I settled back into the familiar rotation of training days, alert days, and then a day off to spend with the family. In the off-hours, we went exploring with the kids, and I even bought a motorcycle that we enjoyed riding through the countryside.

During this time, the Korean War was being fought directly to the west of Japan. Pusan, South Korea, is just 100 miles west of Japan at the closest point, and both the Koreans and the Chinese were historical rivals of the Japanese, having suffered greatly at the hands of the Japanese military through the centuries. Therefore, tension was high in the entire region. Also, Russia had recently detonated its first nuclear device, making it America's chief military rival in the world, and Russia and Japan had grievances going back more than a century. With the Russian mainland less than 200 miles from where we were stationed, our training missions and alert days took on a much more urgent feeling than they had in Chicago. As part of the treaty ending World War II, Japan had agreed to demilitarize, which left them vulnerable to hostile attacks from their neighbors. America had assumed responsibility to protect the islands as part of the agreement. That's why we were there.

In those early days of the cold war, the Russians did frequent fly-bys of the Japanese territorial limit. Except for a clearly defined (and fairly narrow) perimeter around each nation, any airplane from any nation is free to fly in international waters. The Russians would launch out of their bases near Vladivostok and fly toward Japan. As they approached the Japanese territorial limit, they would usually break off and avoid entering Japanese airspace. Every so often, they would fly across the island of Hokkaido, violating Japanese sovereignty, which prompted an alert in which we raced to catch them in what was acknowledged to be a hostile act. But the island was so small that by the time we could catch them, they were back out over international waters and safe from retaliation. Our leaders cautioned us never to provoke an incident in open waters, but we pilots ached to catch them in domestic air space so we could fire on them. After all, they were the ones provoking an incident, and it was impossible to know which flight would be the one that might be the initial assault of a conventional or nuclear attack. These thoughts kept our nerves on edge most of the time we were flying.

On one occasion, some of my buddies were pulling alert when they were scrambled to intercept a Russian BULL (a large bomber, similar to our B-29) that had entered restricted airspace, and they took after him like crazy. He'd strayed (or purposely penetrated) farther than usual, and our boys were able to catch him while he was still over Hokkaido. They brought him into their sights, got a firm lock, and requested permission to fire on what at that moment was a hostile intruder. They could have easily shot him down, proving that the Russians were taunting Japan and defying their sovereignty. As fate would have it, the flight controller was an inexperienced second lieutenant, and he didn't know what to say. So he did what controllers always do—he instructed our pilots to stand by.

The pilot radioed back, "You need to make a decision pretty quick, or we'll lose him!"

About that time, the division commander came into the command post. In a matter of moments, he'd reviewed the situation and issued the order to fire. But, within just those few seconds of hesitation, the Russian airplane had ducked into some clouds for cover, and the pilots lost visual contact. It was too risky to fire strictly on radar; there was the off chance that the missile would go astray and damage other traffic in the area. Before our guys could get a good sight on him again, he'd managed to escape to the safety of international waters, and we had to break off the attack. That's how quickly things happen in the air.

There were a number of times that our pilots did get the chance to play games with the Soviets. One day a brand new Russian TU-4 medium-range bomber flew out of Vladivostok and headed for Chitose. When the Russian figured out that we'd scrambled on him, he went to full thrust to get the heck out of our airspace, while our commander and an operations officer in a second F-86 flew at full blazes to catch him. They did intercept him, but only after he was safely back in open airspace. Disappointed with the pursuit, our guys decided to have some fun. They flew under the belly of the bomber and took some pictures, then rolled out to the top to take more pictures. They flew off his wing, trying to catch a glimpse of his face and gesture at him. All of this was designed to provoke the pilot or a member of the crew in the hopes that he'd shoot at them, because if the Russians initiated a hostile act our guys could engage him. But the Russian pilot kept his cool and allowed them to do their fly-bys, all the while heading back toward the safety of the Russian mainland. By the time our commander and his wing broke off to head for home, they were low on fuel, so they had to stop at an intermediate field on the island of Honshu for refueling before coming back to base. When they arrived at Chitose, they were so happy and pleased with themselves they wanted to celebrate.

After about a year in Japan, an opportunity opened up for us to move to a much more comfortable house in Sapporo, fifteen miles north of Chitose. The move required me to commute to work, but it provided my family a much nicer environment to live in. We loved the area, particularly since it had a beautifully groomed golf course where Realla and I got to play together fairly regularly. After resettling, I was asked to serve as the Scoutmaster for the American troop organized by our church, an assignment I thoroughly enjoyed. In addition to our regular Sunday meetings, I met with the Scouts each week to go through the regular curriculum and advancement. One of our merit badges focused on the live trapping of animals, and the boys decided they wanted to set some snares out in the forested area near our homes. Initially, they made small traps and caught some squirrels and birds. Then they decided to practice making some big traps, even though there weren't really any animals of that size to capture. It was an interesting exercise. The six boys in my troop busily set about studying how to make the various snares. Eventually they learned how to pull a branch down on a sapling tree, set a hook on it, and then camouflage it so it was well hidden in the undergrowth. We set the traps, returned home, and went on to other activities.

A few days later, I got a call from the wing commander, summoning me to his office. It sounded like something was wrong, but he didn't tell me what it was until I got there.

"Fisher, are you a Scoutmaster?"

"Yes, sir."

"Apparently you've been setting traps out in the forest."

I gulped. "Yes, sir, we were practicing a merit badge."

"Well, I've been called to task by the Japanese army. It seems you've caught some of their soldiers in your traps, and they're not happy about it!"

It was all I could do not to laugh. For that matter, it was all the wing commander could do not to laugh. I tried to think of the correct thing to say, but words eluded me.

"Don't set any more traps, Fisher—is that understood?"

"Yes, sir—no more traps."

One of the things that impressed us was how much the Japanese love fireworks. I doubt that there's any place in the world that has more fireworks per capita than in Japan, with the possible exception of China. One day Realla and I were walking downtown when I said casually, "My kid brother sure would love some of these fireworks." I thought they would be a lot of fun for him, back in Idaho, but I didn't think anything more about it. About three or four days later, I was surprised to see four officers standing on the tarmac as I landed my aircraft at the conclusion of a training mission. I parked the airplane and dismounted to find out what was up. It looked pretty serious, since the squadron commander, the chief of operations, and the judge advocate general and one of his assistants were all waiting for me. I saluted, waiting to find out what they wanted, but the squadron commander just said, "Give your parachute and flying gear to the crew chief, and he'll take care of it for you while you come with me."

We went over to the commander's office.

"Fisher, we have reason to believe you've sent some

fireworks through the mail, and they exploded." I'm sure my face flushed.

"With all due respect, sir, I haven't sent any fireworks to anyone."

"Then how do you explain this?"

He showed me a picture of an exploded package, with fragments all over the place. As I studied it more closely, I could see what appeared to be our home address written in the beautiful handwriting of my wife. I got a sick feeling in my stomach.

"Sir, it appears that we may have done that. May I please use the phone to provide an explanation?" Permission was granted, so I dialed Realla.

"You didn't send a package through the mail recently, did you?"

"I sent one to your brother the other day with some little cracker balls that you throw on the ground to explode. Why, is something wrong?"

I'm sure the tone of my voice was pretty solemn.

"We're not supposed to ship anything with explosives in it."

"But certainly cracker balls aren't considered explosives?"

I explained that there was a problem and said, "Let me find out what happened, and I'll call you back."

It turned out that the package had nearly 100 of these small cracker balls in it, each wrapped securely in paper. Realla had also taken pains to write "Handle with Care" on the outside of the wrapping. In spite of that, when the package reached Tokyo, one of the workers decided to reinforce her message by stamping "Fragile" on it. When he brought the stamp down, the package exploded. I felt awful.

"I'm very sorry, sir, that I did this, and I'll be glad to pay for any damages. I hope no one was hurt."

I think it took them by surprise that I accepted responsibility in that fashion. As an officer, I was responsible not only for my own actions but also for those of my family. They told me that the postal worker hadn't been seriously hurt, other than having the wits scared out of him. Still, they indicated they'd have to write up an Article 15, which is a letter of reprimand that stays in your file for a minimum of one year. If there are no further incidents, they remove the letter at that time. The biggest problem with an Article 15 is that while it's in your file, you're not eligible for promotion.

They wrote up the Article 15 but never mailed it. I wondered why, but I didn't want to raise the question with anyone. Then, a few weeks later, a good friend of mine came up to me and said quietly, "You wouldn't want to have this in your record, would you?" He showed me the Article 15.

"Where'd you get that?" I asked indignantly.

He smiled a devious smile. "I was walking past the wing commander's office one day and nobody was in there, but this was on his desk, so I thought I'd better pick it up. I don't think he missed it, since he transferred out a couple of days later, and I think he had more important things on his mind." I must have looked concerned or guilty, because he reassured me that no one cared, particularly since it would come out of the file anyway.

The closest I ever came to combat on assignment in Japan was when we received permission to take an extended flight over to Korea. The 4th Tactical Wing that I was assigned to had originally been assigned to Korea, but it had moved its base of operations to Hokkaido shortly before I arrived. It was within our range of operations to fly over there. We flew cross-country from Chitose to Honshu and over the water to Tachikawa for a final refueling before crossing into Korea.

Two of us were flying in a T-33, and after crossing the Sea of Japan and entering Korean air space, we headed for a base identified as K-55 where we could land and refuel. When we got to the area where the base should have been, there was adverse weather at about 20,000 feet. Normally that wouldn't have been any problem, but as we got ready to land we couldn't raise anyone on the radio. After fussing with the controls, we figured out that our radio was on the blink, so we had no way to communicate with the base on our assigned frequency. As we tried to figure out what to do, we continued heading north at a fairly high rate of speed. Suddenly we heard a burst of static from the radio, followed by an urgent voice on an emergency frequency.

"Aircraft headed north of K-55. This is Scranton Radar Site. Turn south immediately as you've crossed the DMZ [demilitarized zone] and are in unfriendly territory! Repeat, aircraft headed north of K-55, turn south and return to friendly territory."

We headed south as fast as we could, back to K-55. But with only the emergency radio, we couldn't request clearance to land at the nearest airbase, so we continued to Suwan Air Base, where we descended through the clouds and, without authorization, made a visual approach and landed. Once on the ground, we refueled and headed back for Japan. Thus, I flew a combat aircraft in Korea but didn't encounter any combat.

Even though we were in a noncombat zone, tragedies still occurred. On one assignment we were ordered to practice firing live ordnance.[1] A group of us loaded our aircraft with rockets and headed down to Misawa to a military range in the ocean where we could go out and fire. It was a bitter cold winter, and we all wore the Mark IV survival suit made out of latex, with cords around the arms and legs to cinch the openings closed to keep out water and cold. Chuck Wiggins was one of the pilots assigned to the exercise, and somehow he got a knick in his survival suit, so he left it at the base to be repaired and wore just a regular flight suit. When it came time to fire his rockets on the range, he did everything right and pulled the trigger at the precise moment. Unfortunately, the rocket pod hadn't fully descended, and the rockets fired directly into the belly of his aircraft, tearing up and burning all the hydraulic lines. Between the fire and loss of hydraulics, he simply couldn't control the plane through the stress of a landing, and he had to bail out over the ocean.

The water was ice cold—in fact there were large icebergs floating in the water—and Chuck rapidly developed hypothermia. We radioed for help immediately. There was a helicopter in the vicinity, but it couldn't rescue Chuck because the water was so rough. The pilot was afraid he couldn't get close enough to make a rescue without endangering his

1. *Ordnance* is the military term for military weapons of all kinds with their equipment, ammunition, and so on.

own aircraft. Chuck remained in the freezing water until an HU-16 survival rescue aircraft came out and landed in the water, where they picked him up. The waves were so high that the pilot couldn't get the aircraft back up into the air—he just used his power to plow through the water to taxi to shore. The crew got Chuck out and transferred him to an ambulance, but it was too late; he died from exposure. Chuck's wife stayed with us for a couple of days while the Air Force made arrangements for his funeral. It was devastating for all of us.

Eventually, I received a promotion to captain with a change in responsibility to flight commander. Because of my new leadership responsibility, they wanted me to move back to Chitose from Sapporo to be just minutes away in case something needed my attention. This time, they provided on-base housing in our own Quonset hut, which was convenient for me but not as enjoyable for my family.

By this time, we were fully integrated into the local culture and enjoyed the many friends we'd made, both on the base and in the community. My family was quite relaxed in Japan, and we moved easily among the local people. On one occasion, I lost track of my oldest son, Brad, in the middle of a crowd in the center of Chitose during a local celebration. The streets were very crowded, which increased my anxiety. I noticed that the crowd seemed to be congregating at one end of the street, but there were so many people I was having a hard time seeing what was going on. As I tried to wriggle my way through the crowd to find Brad, a Japanese doctor approached me and asked if I was looking for my son. When I told her that I was, she smiled and said, "Well look out there in the middle of the crowd and you'll find him." I wasn't prepared for what I saw next. The reason the crowd had gathered was that there was a sumo wrestling ring in the center, with two huge sumo wrestlers getting ready to fight each other. The sumos are treated with great regard in Japan and are something of national and regional heroes. There, in the middle of the ring, was my son Brad, humbly bowing to one of the sumo wrestlers, who then pretended to wrestle with Brad—even to the point of letting him win! Brad was about seven years old at the time, and the crowd loved it. I couldn't help but laugh and took him triumphantly from the ring so they could get on with the real wrestling. It was interesting to me that the Japanese, who are generally a small people—about my size (it's the one place in the world where I'm considered average height)—love these giants of men who train diligently for their entertainment.

It was shortly after our transfer back to Chitose that the Korean War came to an end, which was great news for America and for all the men who were in combat. But the end of the war had some serious consequences for those of us who were full-time military. When a war ends, you suddenly have far more personnel than are required to maintain a peace-time military, so the military begins a Reduction-in-Force (RIF). That means if they have 100 active-duty pilots, they might let 50 of them go. A lot of men who were about ready to retire from the service took this as an opportunity for early retirement. More were simply reassigned to non-pilot roles, such as BX officers (base-exchange). In other words, they went from being a pilot to being a supply officer.

It was discouraging for someone who had invested all the time required for flight training to suddenly be grounded.

I was very nervous about what was going to happen to me. Then a letter arrived instructing me to transfer to Malstrom Air Force Base in Great Falls, Montana. The heart-breaking news about my next assignment had finally arrived. I would have complained, but the line of unhappy pilots was already too long, and my duty was to go where the Air Force needed me. We made arrangements to pack our belongings and move back to the United States.

CHAPTER FIVE

DARK DAYS IN MONTANA

PERHAPS YOU'VE SEEN THE large bubble-shaped structure that can be seen near any major airport. Sometimes they're located on the crest of a tall mountain, such as the one near Hill Air Force base in Utah, close to where I grew up. The bubble houses sophisticated radar equipment used to track all flights within a designated radius, providing the information needed by GCI (Ground Control Intercept) to scramble alert aircraft if an unidentified or hostile intruder enters the airspace. My orders were to report to the GCI at Malstrom, where I would work in the radar control field. About the last thing in the world I wanted to do was sit passively at a video display watching for intruders while some other pilot got to fly the alert to intercept them. It was discouraging even to think about, and I fell into something of a dark mood as we arrived in Montana.

After going to radar school, I checked into the Canadian Club, the call sign assigned to our radar installation. The people were good to work with, except for a major at the 29th Air Division who went out of his way to make things difficult for us. He was a grounded navigator who had the attitude that if he had to stay on the ground, everyone else should too. When I took my papers down to headquarters to get the promised time flying F-89J's, he told me they had "more pilots than we can shake a stick at, and there's no way we can keep them all current on their flying." Rather than give me even the bare minimum allotted, just four hours per month, he suggested I go to one of the other units on the base and see if they could use me. That wasn't what I'd been promised, and it just added to my unhappiness with the whole situation.

I did go down to the base flight section, however, and checked out in the L-20 DeHavilland Beaver. It's a single-engine propeller aircraft used mostly by bush pilots in Canada. It's a sturdy airplane that the Air Force used to fly support missions in remote areas of Montana. One of this unit's responsibilities was to fly maintenance personnel out to the remote radar sites that could be reached only by air. It was enjoyable flying the airplane, but there were two problems with this assignment. First, it wasn't a jet fighter, and second, there was no compensation for flying these after-hour missions.

I became a little obsessed about flying because I actually logged more flying hours on the L-20 than I did while flying full-time in Chicago and Japan. One month, I logged in sixty hours as a volunteer—a higher number of hours than the pilots assigned to the unit. That was mostly because I'd accept difficult flights that no one else wanted to take. In retrospect, that service came at the expense of my family, because I was tired most of the time and spent a great deal of time away from home flying these extra uncompensated missions. It wasn't unusual to get off work at the site at 17:00, take a flight into the bush that didn't get home until 01:00 the following morning, only to be back to work at 08:00. Realla was amazingly patient, probably because she knew how disappointed I was with how things were working out, but it was a strain on her.

One night, after attending a church social with the family, the phone rang with a request for me to fly a special part into a radar site about 200 miles east of Great Falls. It was an emergency because one of the radar towers had been damaged, and they were worried that the high winds would tear the fabric of the bubble and force them to shut down the site. I was tired but told them okay. I took off about midnight on one of the coldest nights on record (the outside temperature indicator showed minus 40 degrees Fahrenheit). Even with the engine running at full power, the interior of the aircraft was freezing cold. The heater couldn't compensate, so I zipped my heavy winter parka up around my neck with the collar up, covering my nose, and Itucked my flight suit around my legs to try to keep them warm. I worried that the engine might actually have trouble functioning in the frigid air, and I planned that, if necessary, I'd land near a haystack and set it on fire to avoid freezing to death. Fortunately, the engine worked perfectly, and the flight proceeded without any problem.

As the wheels touched down at the radar site, the airport manager came running out to me, waving his arms while yelling, "Don't shut it down! Don't shut it down!"

That was an unusual request, since I would need to refuel before heading back home, but I left the engine idling while he crawled into the cabin to talk with me. "I've got three airplanes over there that shut their engines down, and we can't get them started back up again. If you let your engines stop for even a moment, you're going to be stuck here."

"How can you refuel the airplane for the return trip?"

"Don't worry, we've developed a procedure where we can safely refuel even with the engine running."

And that's just what he did. It was really amazing to experience weather conditions that harsh. After unloading the parts, I took off and made it back home just as the sun was breaking over the horizon and it was time for me to go to work at the GCI site. I did my duty that day but was so mentally exhausted when I got home that night I wanted to cry. But I didn't stop flying extra missions.

About a year later, they asked me to take an L-20 aircraft to Minneapolis, Minnesota, for its 1,000-hour maintenance and rebuild and then fly home by commercial aircraft. I was to fly in winter conditions, with skis on the airplane so I could take off and land in the snow. The first hop was to a refueling point about midway to Minneapolis. While I was munching down a sandwich, a couple of fellows approached me to say they were trying to get home on an emergency leave and hoped to get a ride as far as Minneapolis. I said sure, so the three of us took off for the next leg of the journey. Unfortunately, we ran into some adverse weather that blew us off course. The L-20 travels only about 130 miles per hour, which makes it particularly vulnerable to high winds. It was difficult to keep track of the aircraft's position, and at one point we lost the radio beacon to Minneapolis. That was a serious problem, because it meant we were entering restricted airspace as an unidentified aircraft, and it was likely they'd scramble some jets to check me out. While it wasn't likely they'd take hostile action, the incident would certainly get written up and look bad on my record.

Flying by dead reckoning, I managed to find the lights of Minneapolis but couldn't locate Holden Field. The air was so bitter cold that ice crystals were obscuring our vision. Fighting the high winds had burned more fuel than usual. The gauge barely registered any fuel, and the tanks were awfully light. Our possible flight time was down to just minutes. I kept heading toward the point where the field should be when the red alarm light came on to signal the tanks were empty. It was about 23:00 at night with a strong wind blowing.

There was nothing to do but pull back on the power, shut the engine down, and start gliding in for an emergency landing. It's amazing how many thoughts can crowd through your mind at a time like that: *Where should we land? What are we going to hit? What's the safest way to land to avoid damaging the aircraft and hurting the passengers on board?* No matter how hard I peered out the window, though, I couldn't see any place that looked safe to land. Then, as we closed on the ground, there was a dark area with no lights, so I decided to head in that direction. At least we wouldn't crash into any buildings occupied by people. As we got closer and closer to the ground, I saw a car pass underneath us, and I thought at the very least we could land on the road, even if it meant losing a wing if we hit a telephone pole on the side of the road. I lined up with the car and was about to set it down when the car taillights disappeared for a moment. To my horror I realized that the car had gone beneath an underpass and that we'd hit the top of the underpass if I didn't change course immediately. So I turned back in the direction of the dark area. As the ground came clearly into view, it looked like we were on track to land in a large canal, approximately forty feet wide and twenty feet deep. I held my glide as long as possible before settling down on the icy bank of the empty canal. It was really about the best place I could have found, given the circumstances. We hit the ground with the skis and skidded down the runway with the aircraft twisting and turning in the snow until we stopped just short of a fence. A police car raced up to us with lights flashing, and two security guards got out looking pretty serious.

Before they could say anything I asked, "Where in the world did we land?" I'm sure my voice was trembling, because my legs felt like jelly after the near crash with the underpass.

"You landed in the Twin Cities Arsenal, Minneapolis, Minnesota. Is everyone okay?"

My passengers climbed out and slapped me on the back, congratulating me for getting us down safely, but I felt terrible inside. They thought I'd done a great thing, but in fact I'd done a very foolish thing by running out of fuel.

The police took us to the arsenal's base of operations, and I called home to Great Falls and talked to my boss. He was very angry and said in no uncertain terms, "You get that airplane out of there and get home here as quick as you can."

The next morning, I arranged for a truck to take me back to the aircraft to put enough gas in the wing for the short hop to Holden Field. I was embarrassed to find out that our landing had made it into the local newspaper, which made me feel extremely discouraged. It was one of the darkest days of my career.

After dropping the aircraft off at Holden, I caught a commercial flight back to Gore Field near Great Falls and went in to report to the L-20 squadron commander. He was so angry he said that if he had his way, I'd never fly again. I tried to explain myself, but he wasn't willing to listen. The fact that other lives were endangered added to the seriousness of my mistakes.

He followed through on his threat and filed twenty-one violations—virtually everything he could think of. The only positive thing was that I was assigned a really sharp lawyer who helped out a lot. As we went through each of the charges, he told me to admit to anything that was outside my control, like the weather, and to deny the charges that were more frivolous in nature. He also helped me write a letter of apology for getting into that circumstance. With his advice and the colonel's over-reaction (twenty-one charges were way more than the situation called for), I was allowed to stay on active duty with an Article 15 posted to my file.

When I dragged into work at the GCI site after the hearing, I got a lot of support from coworkers. A lot of people felt that my local commander was being really unfair to me and the other inactive pilots by denying us the opportunity to get our flying hours the regular way. My problems on the Minneapolis flight brought matters to a head, and after two and a half years our fortunes took a turn for the better. We finally got the chance to fly the T-33 jet aircraft for at least four hours per month.

I also volunteered to fly executive officers out on assignment, without compensation, which enabled me to form friendships with some of the leadership at the base. When the Air Force announced a little later that they were going to diminish the size of the GCI site and make an automatic radar site out of it, everyone had to get reassigned to new positions. One of the executives I'd flown around was the division personnel officer, and we'd become pretty good friends. Because of that, he helped me get transferred back to active duty as a pilot. At long last my exile was over, and I was back in the air full-time. I was made a flight commander right off, with responsibility to supervise six to eight pilots. That meant no more volunteer missions, which was a huge relief to my family and me.

The training was very interesting, because we had to prepare for something new—how to deliver nuclear weapons if called on to do so during an alert. My flight group was using F-101s, which are somewhat tricky to fly. We didn't fly with live rockets on our training missions, but we simulated launching them in our practice. It was serious business, since the alert aircraft carried live nuclear weapons. I was grateful each day that went by that we didn't get scrambled and ordered to use the nuclear weapons.

In our after-hours, many of us joined an Aero Club to get in some private flying time. Most of us paid an initiation fee and a monthly membership fee, but the maintenance guys (most of whom were also pilots) could exchange their labor and know-how to maintain the aircraft instead of paying dues.

The club rented a Piper PA-22 four-seater from a base operator in Great Falls. He made it available to us as often as possible, but it seemed like he'd have a charter flight on many of the weekends when most of our guys wanted to fly. Also, the rental cost was so high we couldn't afford to rent it as often as we would have liked.

With about twenty-five pilots in our group clamoring for flying time, it seemed like we could never get enough time to make everyone happy. As the scheduling got worse, I suggested that somebody in the group ought to purchase an airplane so we could control it ourselves.

That idea turned around on me pretty fast when someone said, "Bernie, why don't you buy us an airplane? The dues should be enough to cover the cost, and you can rent it to us."

Everybody applauded the idea—except me. I didn't really want to buy an airplane, but the group desperately needed somebody to step up, so I ended up buying a used PA-22 that belonged to the Aero Club in Glasgow, Montana. They were getting a bigger and faster airplane and were willing to sell this one at a good price. The biggest expense in owning an airplane is the cost of insurance, so one of our members calculated that our Aero Club would need to guarantee forty flying hours per month to cover the cost of insurance, gasoline, and parts for maintenance. In addition, those with mechanical ability should help with maintenance to keep labor costs as low as possible. It was great to have an additional aircraft for the club, and I enjoyed taking my family up flying on an occasional excursion.

By this time I was thinking about airplanes all the time, so I continued to keep my eye out for any good deals that might come along. I soon found an old J-3 Cub in Spokane, Washington, on one of my assigned flights to that area. It had a lot of time on it and needed a full engine rebuild, but the owner wanted to sell it pretty badly, so I asked him if he'd accept a certain price. "No," he said.

"That's okay," I replied, "but if you change your mind, give me a call. Here's my number in Montana."

It was only about two weeks later when he called.

"I've decided I want a new airplane right now, so if you want this one, you can have it." It was a terrific price, so I made the decision to go for it. After writing a check for $700, I climbed into my new acquisition to fly it back to Montana.

Even though it was the beginning of spring, the weather was still pretty uncertain. I filed a flight plan from Spokane to Great Falls across the snow-covered mountains of the Idaho Wilderness area, which left me on my own in some extremely rugged country. The airplane flew without a problem, although I had to set down once at a small unmanned airport that didn't even have a shed. They'd driven a snowplow on a single swath down the middle of the runway, so I set the airplane down in the trough they'd created. The snow was almost touching under both wings, and when I reached the end of the runway, there wasn't enough room to even turn the airplane. I had to pick up its tail and pivot 180 degrees for takeoff. I made the final hop to Great Falls and landed at the airport. The next challenge was to get the airplane over to my house, where we planned to work on it in the garage. It was going to cost a lot of money to hire a truck to haul the airplane, but that seemed like the only way to get it there. My radar observer suggested that with a headwind holding steady at around forty miles per hour, he thought we could land it right in my backyard by bringing it directly into the wind and reducing air speed to match the headwind. This was kind of unorthodox but an interesting challenge. So we tried it. I approached the backyard at the lowest speed that would maintain flight, pulled the power back, and just rode the current down. It didn't roll more than five feet when it touched the ground. It was one of the most beautiful things you've ever seen. Some local school children thought I must have crashed because the landing was so short, but I was able to wave and assure them everything was okay.

We took the wings off and moved the fuselage into the garage to rebuild the engine. The boys loved having the airplane at the house, since they could let their friends sit in the cockpit and pretend to fly it. Working on the airplane was an enjoyable way to relax, and it gave me time to be with the boys since I was doing the work at home.

In addition to renting to the Aero Club, I also used these private airplanes to help our local elders quorum raise money. Periodically we'd have an outing where I'd volunteer to take people up for fifteen-minute flights, and I'd donate the price of admission to the church. It was fun for the local members to get to fly in an airplane, and I enjoyed acting as their chauffeur.

After five years in Great Falls, I was due for rotation.

Word came that the Air Force was going to send us to Homestead Air Force base in Florida, so I sold the two airplanes and got the family ready for a transfer. I think the early years in Montana were the darkest days of my life and certainly the hardest in our marriage. Realla was so patient and supportive even though I was away for many hours. Things brightened considerably when I got back up in the sky as part of my regular duty and I could stop the extra flights for other divisions. I also got some harsh-weather flying that challenged my skills and taught me to always stay sharp. With the hundreds of hours of flying time I logged in all types of propeller and jet aircraft, I was a far more experienced pilot than when I had arrived in Montana. It was May 1962, and the future seemed full of promise.

CHAPTER SIX

FLYING A DEAD-STICK IN FLORIDA

IN SPITE OF THE FACT THAT we'd made a lot of friends in Montana, the family was pretty excited to go to Florida. Homestead Air Force Base is approximately twenty miles south of Miami, so we were going from one of the coldest spots in the country to one of the warmest.

The best news from my point of view was that I'd be flying the new Lockheed F-104 Starfighter, one of the most amazing airplanes ever built. With a fuselage that's fifty-eight feet long and wings just seven and a half feet wide, it looks more like a rocket than an airplane, particularly on a steep angle of ascent. The thin, swept wings create almost no drag, making the aircraft highly maneuverable. In fact, the leading edges of the wings have a radius of just 0.0016 inches, which is so sharp they have to be covered while the aircraft is on the ground to prevent people from cutting themselves.

In many respects the F-104 was way ahead of its time, and pilots loved it, even though it was difficult to control. Normal cruising speed is 525 miles per hour, but it can easily approach Mach 2 without hesitation and can actually exceed Mach 2 for short durations. The fastest I ever flew the airplane was just shy of Mach 2, which is the point when a red warning light advises you to back off because of the excess heat that builds up on the engine mounts. Even though the outside air temperature is lower than minus 60 degrees Fahrenheit at cruising altitude, there were times flying faster than Mach 1 when I took my gloves off and put my hand on the windshield to feel the intense heat that the friction creates at that speed.

It's an interesting sensation to fly at extremely high rates of speed. When you're safely off the ground and at altitude, you engage the afterburner to provide full thrust. The speed of sound is 720 miles per hour (Mach 1). As the aircraft reaches approximately 650 miles per hour, it begins to shudder from the resistance, and you can feel a noticeable drag on your acceleration. Then, as you cross the sound barrier, you feel like you've broken through a bubble—the resistance disappears and the aircraft seems to jump forward with virtually no drag. The only sensation of speed is that the airplane seems to do a little dance with a slight shiver on the controls. If you accelerate just a little faster all movement disappears, and it's the smoothest feeling in the world—the engine is operating efficiently, and there's very little sound. At Mach 1.3 the air seems to swell a bit, slowing your acceleration until you burst through 1.4, where the aircraft moves out faster. At 1.7 the engine goes into a high-speed position, making you feel as if someone just gave you a quick boot in the tail as the increased thrust throws you back against your seat—and away you go. Finally, as you approach Mach 2, the engine gets so hot the red light comes on to tell you that you're going fast enough. My understanding is that test pilots have flown the F-104 up to Mach 2.3, but at that point the glass gets so hot it tends to dish out, creating a dangerous flying condition. I personally never pushed it beyond the red light.

Our patrol area included the Gulf of Mexico, the northern Caribbean to St. Thomas, and east to the Bahamas. Because of the communist regime in Cuba, there was a lot of tension, with frequent active alerts. After Castro's recent takeover of Cuba, many people tried to escape using small boats to cross the Straits of Florida. The Cuban navy fired on them when possible, so we often flew interference for the escapees. On one occasion, we received a report that there was a large Russian ship in the area, and I was scrambled to investigate. I think they wanted to implicate the Russians in interfering with escaping Cubans. When I arrived on the scene, however, there were no Cuban boats in the area, so I reported back to Flight Control that there was no problem. Still, they ordered me to get the ship's registry, perhaps to harass the Russians a bit. Russian numbers are hard to read, so I had to fly past several times before I could call out all the numbers to my wingman. The Russian ship was one of the most beautiful I'd ever seen—tan with sharp lines and a striking silhouette. I passed by at the lowest speed I could maintain (approximately 140 miles per hour), and at 100 feet off the water I was close enough to see the Russian sailors waving cheerfully at me.

On another occasion, I was scrambled to fly an intercept on a commercial airliner coming out of Mexico City. The pilot was off his flight plan; he showed up as an unidentified potential intruder. The night was dark, making it easy to come up on him unobserved. Judging from the lights in the passenger windows, it was obviously a commercial flight, but my military controllers wanted his tail number to identify which flight it was. So I slid in between the wing and the tail, very close to the fuselage, and I looked right down into the windows of the airliner. I could see the passengers' faces through the windows, although none of them turned to look at me. I got the airliner's tail number, called it in, and then slipped out unobserved to return to base. I don't believe either the pilot or any of the passengers had any idea they'd been intercepted by a military aircraft.

One of the most important events of the period occurred while I was on duty at Homestead—the Cuban Missile Crisis of 1962. As we arrived at the base one morning, we were summoned to a special briefing to inform us that they'd increased the number of alert planes on duty and that we'd been loaded with a full complement of live ordnance. We flew our regular missions during the seventeen days of the crisis, but fortunately we were never scrambled to actually engage the enemy. It was obvious that the president was serious in what he was doing, and the military was prepared to back him up if he gave the order to attack.

Part of the provocation for the Cuban Missile Crisis was that America was flying U-2 spy planes at extremely high altitudes over Cuba to take pictures and monitor Cuban activities. That really provoked the communist government of Fidel Castro. Sometimes we'd be asked to meet a returning U-2 and escort him back to base. Although the F-104 couldn't climb as high as the U-2, we could get up to some very high altitudes (test pilots made it above 70,000 feet), and we were allowed to run intercepts on the returning U-2 to improve our skills. To handle the altitude this exercise required, we needed a special pressurized flight suit that could respond to the terrific pressure exerted on our bodies during those high-altitude maneuvers. It was exciting to test one's personal endurance in such extreme conditions.

Most Air Force pilots go their entire career without having to make a forced landing with no power. You practice them just in case, because at an altitude of 3,000 or 4,000 feet and a cruising airspeed of more than 500 miles per hour, there's not a lot of time to react if something goes wrong. The problem with these "simulated flame-out" practice runs (usually made when you're returning to base with a little extra fuel left over) is that you always pull out at the last moment of the drill to avoid hitting the ground too hard and causing damage to the undercarriage of the aircraft. No matter how much you study or practice for it, it's impossible to fully prepare for an actual emergency landing. As you log in hundreds of missions without mechanical failures, the possibility of ever having to make a real "dead-stick" landing seems increasingly remote. Perhaps that's why it was such a surprise the first time I smelled an odd, acrid odor in the cockpit that told me something was wrong even before anything registered on the instrument panel. I was flying practice missions with three other fighters running intercepts on each other over the Gulf of Mexico at the time.

Even though the instruments gave no indication of a problem, an alarm went off in my mind when the odor persisted, and I instinctively hunched forward to react to whatever was wrong. Then I saw the oil pressure dropping, which signaled a potential engine failure.[1] Fortunately, we weren't that far from the base, so acting on my training, I immediately pulled back on the control stick to increase altitude from 3,000 feet to 10,000 feet. Next, I notified my wingman of the trouble, and he closed range so he could fly next to me to help me through the emergency procedure. The first thing he asked was, "Have you pulled the pins, Bernie?" The pilot's seat is equipped with an explosive charge that blows it free from the aircraft when you have to make a parachute landing, and cotter pins are used to avoid accidentally setting it off while working on the ground. I reached down and checked to make sure, while radioing in a "Mayday" declaring an in-flight emergency. Flight Control confirmed that

---

1. Engine oil pressure serves two vital functions in a jet engine—lubrication and hydraulic pressure to control the jet output nozzle. Visualize the rear nozzle on a jet engine where super-compressed air and fuel shoot out at more than 10,000 pounds of thrust when operating normally. The nozzle is a circular opening at the rear of the jet engine, much smaller than the air intake opening at the front of the engine. As the jet fuel combusts inside the engine, it expands dramatically, which in turn spins a series of fan blades that draw in the huge volume of air needed for combustion. It's this combination of air being sucked into the front of the engine and expelled under pressure from the rear nozzle that gives the aircraft the forward thrust needed to achieve flight.

There are two ways to control and increase the amount of thrust: (1) increase the volume of air going through the engine by using more fuel, or (2) restrict the

they'd initiated the process of clearing the runway for an emergency landing.

At 10,000 feet, I started to turn toward Homestead just as the oil pressure dropped to zero and the rear nozzle went wide open. There was an immediate loss of power, and the aircraft started slowing down. Ground control gave me the instrument settings needed to find the runway, since a storm front moving in from the east had obscured the approach.

If I wasn't lined up perfectly with the runway at 3,000 feet, I'd have to jump and allow the aircraft to crash. I watched the altimeter as the plane slowly descended into the storm front and instinctively tightened my grip on the controls. With reduced power, the turbulence buffeted the aircraft more than usual, increasing my chances of being knocked off course. The seconds ticked by to the sound of an increasing growl from the engine, now spinning without lubrication. I should have shut it down, but I was still too far out to make it to base without power.

At 3,000 feet, I broke through the cloud cover and, much to my relief, could see the runway right where it was supposed

---

diameter of the nozzle so the air and combusted fuel is forced through a smaller hole. Either way, you get more pressure coming out of the tail of the engine. In the normal operating position, the diameter of the rear nozzle is optimized for fuel efficiency and thrust to maintain flight. The diameter of the opening of the nozzle can be adjusted using oil pressure to open and close the nozzle. The more oil pressure the pilot applies to the fins that surround the rear nozzle, the smaller the nozzle opening. The pilot has to keep the nozzle fairly restricted when operating on just the main engine to achieve the right amount of thrust in a fuel-efficient manner. If the engine loses oil pressure, the nozzle opens up and the engine loses power because of the decrease in thrust. That was one of the most immediate risks of an engine failure to be. I felt my shoulders relax and radioed my intention to proceed with the landing. By this time, the sound of the engine bearings had increased to an angry roar, as the internal friction was creating tremendous heat. It was a matter of moments until the metal would start to melt, which would throw the turbines out of balance and cause the blades in the fan to shatter. An explosion was the inevitable outcome.

In the last seconds before total engine failure, I came over the end of the runway and gratefully shut the engine down, drifting onto the runway without power. Contact with the ground was surprisingly smooth, all things considered. As the aircraft streaked down the runway, I applied the brakes in a slow, steady motion since the hydraulics were a bit soggy without power. Fortunately, the F-104 is equipped with antilock brakes that automatically release and then reassert themselves when they sense a skid, thus decreasing ground speed to the point that I could deploy the drag-chute from the aft end of the aircraft to provide additional braking power. The chute grabbed the wind and helped me come to a rather abrupt stop, just short of the swampy ground at the end of the runway. I'd successfully made a dead-stick landing and lived to tell about it!

I let out a terrific sigh of relief as the ground crew raced over to help me out of the aircraft so the emergency landing crews could drag it off the runway and keep the field open for other returning flights. There were cheers all around, and I was treated as something of a hero for bringing the plane down in one piece. I learned later that I was to receive a "Company Point with Pride," a special commendation plaque from the Air Defense Command.

I discussed the problem of losing thrust when the oil pressure drops with some of the other pilots. We thought of an innovative way to provide some extra maneuvering altitude by using the afterburner, which operates with the nozzle open. Our new idea was to immediately light the afterburner when the pilot becomes aware of an oil problem and thus gain maximum thrust to increase altitude prior to the flameout.[2]

With trial and error, we found that the ideal pattern to survive a flameout was to bring the aircraft up to 15,000 feet and then start into a 45-degree descending turn that ultimately results in a full 360-degree twist toward the ground, with the end of the spiral reached at 500 feet—the precise moment to lower the landing gear. Lowering the wheels any earlier would create too much drag on the aircraft and bring it down too fast.

The spiral turn provides greater control over the approach and also gives you the chance to observe your position relative

---

2. The phenomenon of the fins opening with loss of oil pressure produced an opportunity to use the afterburner, which operates with the fins open anyway. Here's the essence of our idea. For takeoff and emergency acceleration, the pilot can engage a secondary engine called the afterburner, which is a small engine mounted behind the main engine. It adds an extra 5,000 pounds of thrust. The afterburner really guzzles fuel, which is why it's used only when maximum thrust is needed. With both engines operating at maximum power, there's too much exhaust to pass through the normal opening of the rear nozzle, so the opening is increased to accommodate the increased volume.

In the normal operation of the aircraft, the pilot controls the nozzle as the afterburner is engaged and disengaged. In an impending engine failure, we decided it would make sense to open the nozzles immediately and engage the afterburner to gain altitude rather than waiting for the nozzles to open by themselves with the corresponding loss of power if only the main engine was in use.

to the runway, which is critical in maintaining the perfect timing needed for a true dead-stick landing. Starting at 15,000 feet provides enough time to check progress at key points in the spiral. For example, at 275 degrees you should be at 7,500 feet. If you're too high, you can slide into a tighter circle and drop down somewhat faster, or if you're too low you can slide out into a wider circle to cover more distance in the next part of the spiral. Of course, airspeed is constant, so it's the amount of distance covered that determines how fast you lose altitude. At the 90-degree point you should be at 3,500 feet, and finally at 1,500 feet you begin to straighten out for the final approach to the runway.

One of the reasons we spent so much time practicing emergency procedures was that the F-104s reliability was proving less than desirable. Our West German allies also flew this aircraft and eventually nicknamed it the "Widow Maker" because of its mechanical problems.

A little less than a year after my first dead-stick landing, I had an even greater challenge while flying over Bimini in the Bahamas islands. Once again, the engine oil pressure started dropping. At first I thought, *This can't be happening!* But I was better prepared this time and immediately went "outboard on the throttle" to engage the afterburner. It was reassuring to feel the remarkable kick that comes from an immediate 50-percent increase in thrust. I wanted to give myself as much room to maneuver as possible.

While simultaneously climbing to gain maximum altitude, I radioed the base for assistance and told them my position. Since Bimini is perhaps seventy miles off the coast, I had enough time to climb to 45,000 feet as I brought myself into position above Homestead. Fortunately, the engine kept operating long enough to bring me over dry land. Covering that much distance with the afterburner engaged used up the oil pretty quickly, but at least it didn't matter that the nozzle was wide open. At 45,000 feet the growling from the engine was so severe that I had no choice but to shut it down.

So there I was, more than nine miles above the ground with no power. To land the aircraft, I would have to make three 360-degree spirals to be on proper approach for the runway. I had never tried it before, and my heart raced at the thought. I successfully deployed the small emergency wind turbine that turns a small generator to give minimum power for instruments and radio, as well as provides some hydraulic pressure. With that minimum amount of power, I felt pretty good—I was in proper position with operational control of the instruments and the aircraft.

Then a new emergency struck. At 45,000 feet the outside air temperature is minus 60 degrees Fahrenheit. With no engine, you lose pressurization on the refrigeration and heating unit, leaving nothing to maintain temperature inside the cabin. Almost immediately everything started to frost over. I was in my flight suit, so I didn't freeze, but somewhere into the second spiral all my controls iced up and the instrument panel disappeared behind a glaze of frost. Worst of all, the canopy of the windshield was completely obscured by frost. Acting on instinct, I continued the second roll, but I couldn't figure out how I'd check my position as I reached each of the predetermined altitudes. Frantically, I searched for something to clear the window, but there was nothing loose in the aircraft. With a small yelp I reached inside my flight suit and pulled out a gasoline credit card, which I used as an ice-scraper to clear a small opening in the window of the aircraft. By leaning as far forward as my safety harness would allow, I could peer through the small opening in the frost to see the runway more than 25,000 feet below. I was a bit shallow at this point, so I widened the arc to compensate. At the end of the second turn, I was still straining to see but had made it almost perfectly to the proper position.

And so I began the third and final spiral. As I got closer to the ground, the heat of the ocean started melting the condensed ice in the cockpit, and in just a few moments there was a small rainstorm. I had a ground speed of about 290 miles per hour, which is really fast. But, in spite of the steepness of my descent, I thought I could get the plane down, so I waived-off on ground control's invitation to bail out. Things were happening so fast at this point that I barely registered the sight of the emergency lights flashing on the rescue vehicles lining the runway. At 500 feet, I engaged the control to drop the landing gear. With the hydraulic pressure at a minimum, it seemed to take much longer than usual, and there was a chance that the wheels might not lock in time. A few seconds later, I hit the ground running much faster than usual. There was a strong jolt, but fortunately the wheels didn't buckle, and I was firmly on the ground. I applied the brakes while holding my finger anxiously over the drag-chute. The temptation to simply release the chute was almost overpowering. But, I knew better. Deploy the chute too quickly and it would be ripped off. Wait too long and the aircraft wouldn't stop in time. So, I waited. At the precise moment I judged optimal I pressed the release, and the chute snapped convincingly behind me, whipping me forward in the seat against my safety restraints, and the aircraft slid easily to a stop. I slowly released my breath, grateful that I'd made it down safely a second time.

Apparently the Air Force thought highly of the maneuver, even though I'd gone against military protocol by landing the aircraft instead of ditching it off the Florida coast, because they gave me my first Air Medal. As I figured it, I'd saved them millions of dollars at that point, which was far more than I would ever cost them in salary during my entire military career. It was a great day.

As I drove home from the base, I couldn't help but smile at the inevitable question that would greet me: "How was your day?" I couldn't wait to tell Realla and the boys. What I couldn't know at that moment was how valuable those two experiences would be in just a little over a year when I'd face combat for the first time in my military career.

PART 2

AT WAR IN VIETNAM

CHAPTER SEVEN

VOLUNTEERING FOR COMBAT

My boys had taken an interest in flying, so I took advantage of a notice posted on a bulletin board indicating that a local pilot was willing to rent his Cessna 172 to qualified pilots. Our two oldest, Brad and Courtney, got pretty accomplished at doing some basic aerobatic maneuvers, including stalls, turns, and dives, even though they were just teenagers. The younger boys preferred to fly straight and level. I enjoyed coaching them and was glad to share my interest in flying with them. Realla loved to fly over the ocean, about ten miles out, where the reef is fairly well built up and you can peer right down into the aquamarine water and see large fish swimming, or maybe even sharks and dolphins.

Florida turned out to be a great place to raise a family, and we took full advantage of all the recreational opportunities available to us. I bought a speedboat that we used in both the ocean and a nearby gravel pit that had filled with water. The boys learned to love waterskiing. On the days that we prepared in advance, we got our routine down to where we could have the boat in the water in less than fifteen minutes from the time I got home. What a great way to spend time together!

We also liked to go exploring in the ocean south of Miami. The John Pennekamp underwater park was within easy driving distance, and we'd often go scuba diving in the area. I used a compressor at the base to fill a couple of oxygen bottles, and away we'd go. I also invented a pair of small water foils that could be towed behind our boat. You'd lie on top of the foil, which had fins on the side and bottom, and when you wanted to dive to see something, you'd just tip the foil forward and the fins would pull you under the water. Of course, the boat had to go pretty slow or the water would rip your face mask off. Sometimes I'd go out with some of the other pilots from the base, but more often a bunch of us would collect our kids and head out. Realla became quite expert at driving the boat while we did our exploring. One day, I spied the kind of green ooze that indicates the presence of brass seeping up from the ocean floor, so I signaled Realla to stop to give me some time to explore the area with scuba gear. As I reached the bottom, I could see the remnants of some old ships. More than 100 years of sediment had pretty well obscured their resting place, but the brass had oozed out of the metal and kind of crawled up on the rocks, giving their location away. We pulled the rocks back and found some pieces of the ship still on the ground. The inscription on some of the brass pieces revealed that there were probably two ships in the area, one British, one Spanish. It was very interesting to explore the old shipwrecks. On another outing, I found an old rusted torpedo that may have wound up there from a training mission, so we hooked a rope to it and towed it to the Navy for disposal.

At church, I was a member of the elder's quorum presidency (which seemed to be the place I was asked to serve most often as we moved around the world), and we started a rather innovative fundraising project. One of the members operated a labor camp, and he told me in passing one day that his men were bothered by swarms of honeybees that formed nests in houses in the area. I suggested that someone should capture the honeybees and create new hives that could be sold to area farmers. "Why not the elder's quorum?" he asked. We put together a committee to study the process, and before I knew it I was a leader in honeybee collection. By the time we left Florida, there were twelve new hives that could be sold for $30 each. I talked with them a year later, and they'd created more than 100 hives, raising more than $3,000 for the quorum. That was a real fortune in 1965.

All in all, Florida was a great experience for our family, and we could happily have stayed there forever. In August of 1964, however, an incident in the Gulf of Tonkin[1] off the coast of North Vietnam prompted Congress to pass a resolution authorizing the president to use force to protect

---

1. Names of Vietnamese sites are taken from the Hammond Vietnam Conflict annotated map, Hammond Incorporated, Maplewood, N.J. For more information on the Vietnam War, see appendix C, "A Brief History of Vietnam and the War."

American interests in Southeast Asia, including Vietnam. Before long, the president initiated bombing raids into North Vietnam as a show of force to get the North Vietnamese military to back off from attacking South Vietnam.

Even though the government of South Vietnam was not popular with its own citizens, it was friendly to the United States, and the president felt it was vital to protect South Vietnam from falling to the communists.[2]

A number of officers who had been stationed as military advisers in Vietnam summoned the pilots in my squadron to a briefing to explain the situation. With the escalating hostilities, there was a growing need for South Vietnamese pilots to fly combat and support missions on an aircraft called the A-1E Skyraider. The premier of Vietnam was an officer in the Vietnamese Air Force and had flown an A-1E on a number of simple missions. He was a flamboyant rascal who wore a purple flying scarf and black flying suit to show his unity with the military. His goal was to build up seven Vietnamese squadrons. To accomplish that, the United States Air Force needed to supply volunteers to work as instructors to train the Vietnamese onsite. The only drawback was that those who volunteered couldn't take their families, since Vietnam was in a combat zone. When no one responded, they asked us to think about it and left.

The next morning, our squadron commander called us all to the briefing room and posed a question: "How many of you have had combat experience?"

---

2. For more a more detailed account of the war, see appendix C, "A Brief History of Vietnam and the War."

Three pilots who had served in Korea raised their hands.

"If the rest of you are going to stay in the Air Force and make a career out of this, you should have some combat experience. There's only one war going on right now, and that's in Southeast Asia. I'm going to recommend that you should put in some time over there. I realize that training on a propeller-driven support aircraft may not be your idea of getting experience, but you need a variety of assignments, including working with foreigners and helping the Air Force honor its commitment to our Allies."

When he finished, five of us raised our hands. Eventually they selected three of us. I went home and told Realla and the family. While there was some natural anxiety about my going into a hazardous area, it seemed like being a trainer would be a fairly safe assignment.

Before I could train others, I had to learn about the aircraft we'd be flying, as well as receive specific training on flying combat-support missions. Accordingly, I started a nine-month regime of training. First was COIN school (counter-insurgency) at Hurlburt field, about 300 miles northwest of Miami in Panama City, Florida. Next was AGOS (Air Ground Operations Support), where we were taught how to coordinate our attacks with Army personnel on the ground. Third was a technical school and certification on the A-1E aircraft. Finally, we needed jungle survival skills and emergency training in case we got shot down. This would be provided during a three-week course in the Philippines.

The family remained at Homestead during the first six months of this training, and I commuted to and from

Hurlburt. Each Monday the Air Force would fly me out on a T-33 to spend the week in intense training and then pick me up on Friday afternoon so we could be with our families. I completed both the COIN and AGOS schools with high scores. It was impractical to fly back and forth during the next three months training on the A-1E, so we moved out of Homestead and into temporary housing in Panama City. I wanted to spend as much time with my family as possible before heading off to a combat area. No on-base housing was available for such a short duration, but we found a small house to rent on an inlet of the Gulf of Mexico. I thought it would be a good experience for the boys to learn something about sailing, so I looked for a small sailboat to rent that we could take out in the inlet and close to the gulf. We found an abandoned boat sitting in the yard of a house in the neighborhood. A quick inspection revealed some work the boat needed to make it seaworthy, particularly replacing some wood that had succumbed to dry rot in the humid Florida air. The owner quoted me a price that was just too good to pass up—so I bought the boat. The boys helped me get it into shape, and then we learned to sail it. It had a small motor in case we ever got stranded, but the boys were remarkably good at maneuvering it. We spent a lot of happy hours together in the evenings and on weekends touring the waterfront.

I came to have a lot of respect for the A-1E. The original A-1 Skyraider had been commissioned as a World War II Navy dive bomber. In the 1950s the Navy used nearly 3,000 Skyraiders in the Korean War. Then, the Air Force decided to deploy a modified version, the A-1E, in Vietnam to provide close ground support. It was a remarkably versatile aircraft, with a single Wright R-3350 radial engine that developed 2,700 horsepower. It could take off and land on a dime and carry an enormous payload (actually greater than the ordnance load of a World War II B-17 bomber, which had four engines and a crew of ten.) You could fit ten men in the back of the fuselage, if needed, but we almost always flew solo to provide more space and carrying capacity for ordnance. In addition to its sizeable bomb payload, it could carry enough fuel to stay airborne up to eight hours. That gave us the ability to stay in a battlefield area for extended periods to provide support to the ground troops. The A-1E had four 20-mm cannons (machine guns) that provided rapid-fire bursts to strafe enemy troop positions or to fire on hostile aircraft, plus a wide variety of bombs, rockets, mines, grenades, flares, and gun pods. It was really something of a versatile mini-arsenal to help the guys on the ground. With a cruising speed of 240 miles per hour, it was nothing like the F-104 Starfighter for speed and acceleration, but it gave pilots lots of opportunity to fly close to the ground, providing a very different kind of excitement. It was kind of a homely airplane, and the joke used to be that the Skyraider "flew faster than the speed of smell." One of my friends, Jump Myers, said it was like flying a dump truck.

As the end of the three-month certification school approached, it was with a heavy heart that I sold our boat and made arrangements for the family to move to Kuna, Idaho. We'd found a small farm to rent very close to Realla's parents, and they promised to help her and the boys in the operation of the farm. After saying good-bye, I caught a commercial flight to San Francisco, then transferred by military transport to Hawaii and on to Clark Field in the Philippines.

The survival skill training was outstanding. They taught us how to locate a particular type of tree in the jungle from which you could drain up to ten gallons of water. We were instructed by some Philippine natives called "Negritos," who were pygmy-sized warriors. The Negritos were ferocious fighters who still used bows and arrows for hunting, and they took us into the jungle to teach us firsthand how to survive. One of the things I remember being taught is how to build a shelter using bamboo and banana leaves. First, jab the bamboo sticks into the ground to build a small frame just big enough for one person and then cover it with a blanket. Next, layer banana leaves over the top of the blanket, folding them to repel the rain. When done properly, such a shelter is virtually leak-proof. Finally, line the entire structure with mosquito netting, which was an absolute miracle in the jungle. More than once I fell asleep with the buzzing of mosquitoes at an almost deafening pitch as they tried to get at me, but the netting kept them out completely. Since the mosquitoes were the single biggest problem I encountered in the jungle, these shelters were wonderful. Without the netting I'm sure the mosquitoes would have eaten me alive as soon as the sun went down.

The Negritos also taught us how to design and deploy trip wires so that if someone tried to come up on us, they'd hit the trip and make a cracking noise that was loud enough to alert us to their presence. One day, while learning how to walk quietly through the jungle, one of our instructors told us that it was not a good idea to travel on the trails—it was better to go out in the foliage where no one had walked before us. To emphasize the point, he took a heavy stick and tossed it a few feet down the trail where it hit a trip, releasing a huge pile of sharpened spikes that had been camouflaged and suspended in the tree above the trip. This deadly load came crashing down with enough force to kill anyone who unwittingly stepped on the trip.

One of the things I had to get used to was the incredible noise of the jungle. Perhaps you've seen movies where the background is constantly filled with the chatter and chirp of jungle animals. In real life it was all that and more.

At the end of the course, the Negritos took us into their village to meet their families. They produced some interesting crafts that they offered for sale. As a way of saying thanks, we purchased some of their goods. I bought a crossbow, a high quality bow-and-arrow, and a beautiful machete.

The course completed, we were cleared for transfer to Vietnam. While it's impossible to fully prepare a person for the emotions and stress of combat, the Air Force had done a terrific job of getting us ready—both physically and mentally—for the challenges that were now upon us. It was with a lot of anticipation and maybe a little anxiety that we boarded a troop transport at Clark Field for transfer to Tan Son Nhut, South Vietnam.

CHAPTER EIGHT

TRAINING THE VIETNAMESE AIR FORCE

MY FIRST IMPRESSION OF Vietnam was formed at Tan Son Nhut Air Base just north of Saigon. I stepped out of the passenger door of the aircraft and into a searing wall of heat that seemed to suck the air right out of my lungs. After living in Florida and training in the Philippines, I still wasn't prepared for the oppressive heat and humidity of the broad Mekong River delta, where the land is flat and rich with flooded rice paddies. It felt like a steam room with no exit. It was obvious from the way the ground crew was attired that our dress blue uniforms and ties made us severely overdressed for the occasion, and the first order of business was to loosen our collars to get some ventilation. When my lungs had time to adjust to the air, I looked around and saw that Vietnam was a beautiful country. Jungle vegetation crowded up against the fences of the air base, and pungent odors gave it an exotic feeling unlike anything I'd experienced before. Perhaps because there's such little slope to the land, water tends to puddle everywhere, contributing to the oppressive humidity.

My second impression was formed as they directed us to a bus for transfer up to our assignment at Bien Hoa. I'd never seen a vehicle like that in my life. All the windows had steel reinforced bars running from front to back, as well as a heavy metal screen protecting each window. The glass windows themselves were rolled down to let in some air, but the screens made it difficult to see inside the bus. We were told that on a couple of occasions a Viet Cong sympathizer had trotted up alongside a bus that was moving slowly through a crowded street and lobbed a grenade inside. The screens were meant to prevent that from happening again. That sounded reasonable, but then another fellow said that the VC had learned to attach a fishhook to a grenade, run up next to the bus, hook the grenade onto the screen, and then run like crazy. For our first hour in Vietnam, that seemed pretty ominous.

It didn't take long to learn that there were five groups of combatants in the war, three official groups and two unofficial. The officially recognized combatants included: (1) the Army of the Democratic Republic of Vietnam North Vietnam (DRV); (2) the Army of the Republic of Vietnam (ARVN), our South Vietnamese allies; and (3) the United Nations forces, led almost exclusively by the Americans.

The fourth group was the Viet Cong, who supported the North Vietnamese. They were by far the most troubling to our troops. Viet Cong (VC) were unofficial but terribly effective soldiers from North Vietnam who traveled down the western border of Vietnam, just inside the boundaries of Laos and Cambodia. They would strike out into South Vietnam to surreptitiously attack military installations and carry out other covert activities. With more than 1,000 miles of border to hide behind, they could strike from almost any direction—north, west, or south—and then retreat back to the safety of Laos or Cambodia, which United Nations policy prevented us from entering. They also recruited South Vietnamese citizens who were disaffected from the corrupt government of the south. So the VC were both North and South Vietnamese guerilla fighters who mingled rather freely with the local population. That created an extremely dangerous situation for those of us who were easily identifiable as foreigners by our appearance and therefore legitimate targets to the Viet Cong. They knew who we were, but we could never know for sure who they were.

The final group of combatants was the Montagnards, so named by the French because they were indigenous "mountain people," and they supported the Americans in the mountainous western regions of the country. They were a great help to our soldiers on the ground, providing aid and assistance when a group got into trouble.

The trip up to Bien Hoa was an uneventful ride on mostly dirt roads. I was surprised at all the foot traffic, with peasants driving their farm animals before them, hundreds of people on bicycles, and pedestrians weaving in and out of traffic. In 1965 America was just starting to expand its presence there, so some of the people were still curious enough that they'd glance at the bus to try to get a look at our faces, but not in an obvious way.

After arriving at Bien Hoa, we made our way to squadron headquarters to check in and sign the roster. We'd arrived on Sunday, so people were pretty relaxed and casual. Eventually they escorted us to our "hooches," which were small wooden housing units covered with a grass roof and mosquito netting sides. Eight of us lived in a hooch, and I was pleased to find that some of the pilots I'd known back in the states were assigned to my living quarters. It made it easier for me to feel comfortable in an unfamiliar setting.

I walked outside just as a helicopter flew overhead with loudspeakers blaring, "LDS Services are at 19:00 hours tonight in the base library."

"You've got to be kidding," I said under my breath, smiling at the thought that I could go to church on my very first day in Vietnam. Some of my buddies came up and slapped me on the back: "Bernie, looks like you've got to go to church tonight."

So I put on my best uniform and walked over to the library. There were about ten people assembled for service, conducted under the direction of Ray Young, an Army captain who flew helicopters. He was the group leader, and he invited us all to come in and sit down. I think we just had a testimony meeting and talked about our families and where we were from, but it was great to be with others who shared my faith. We were also authorized to conduct a sacrament service, which meant a great deal in a combat zone.

Although I wasn't able to attend church as often as I'd have liked because of occasional Sunday flying assignments and missions, I did my best to be supportive of church activities whenever possible. Ray Young was a remarkable man who worked tirelessly to help keep up morale. For example, he volunteered to fly the various military chaplains out to remote locations each Sunday so they could conduct worship services with isolated groups of Americans on field assignment. It didn't matter to him if the chaplain was conducting a Catholic or Protestant service, he made sure they had at least an hour to meet with the troops. When I transferred to a different base a month or so later, Ray would stop by and pick up me and the other LDS guys for church. He even let me fly the helicopter. I wasn't nearly as good with a rotary-wing aircraft (helicopter) as I was with our fixed-wing airplanes, but I did get fairly competent on takeoffs, landings, and basic maneuvers.

Ray did something else that I always admired. Somehow he got it into his head that we ought to have a permanent church rather than having to meet at the library, so he got permission from church headquarters in Salt Lake City to erect a small structure. I'm not sure they were really excited about it, because it would be a challenge to maintain, but it was difficult to resist Ray's enthusiasm. The next step was to raise some money, so we all wrote to our home ward elders quorums to request their help in fund-raising. They were very generous, and in no time we'd raised the money. Finally, Ray needed permission from the Air Force to build a chapel, so he went down to talk with the American wing commander, who turned him down cold. All Ray's skills at persuasion failed him, and he walked out of the office frustrated, having been told that there was absolutely no way that a chapel was going to be built.

It really was impossible to keep Ray down, though. He simply walked a little farther down the road to the next containment area and requested permission to talk to the Vietnamese wing commander, who was the senior ranking officer on the base. Ray went in and explained his idea, and the commander replied that it sounded great. He even assigned Ray a choice plot of ground right next to the library.

The last step was to actually construct the building. At this point we encountered some opposition—one of the Protestant chaplains was very much opposed to the Mormons building a chapel there. He went so far as to threaten to call for a Congressional hearing, and he started raising all kinds of trouble. But that chaplain had a problem—most of us sang in his Protestant choir, and he needed our voices. When he'd start to go off on our proposed chapel, we'd say, "Come on, Chaplain, you wouldn't do that, would you?"

"Yes, I will—there will be hearings on this!"

"But then we couldn't sing in your choir because it just wouldn't seem right."

He wasn't happy about it, but he didn't make any more trouble, and we continued to enjoy singing in his choir.

Ray arranged to have the building prefabricated off-base by a Vietnamese contractor. About three weeks later the building was done. Ray and some volunteers hurried to pour a cement slab on the assigned spot, then brought the chapel in on a truck and attached it to the footings. We had an LDS chapel on the base, complete with a metal faceplate for everyone to see. It wasn't big—just enough to hold about twenty people, but it was still a tangible reminder of home and the things we cared about. It got plenty of use, because we were more than willing to share with people from other faiths, so a lot of church services were held there. Unfortunately, by the time the building was completed, I'd been transferred to a frontline combat unit north to Pleiku, in the central highlands, and I didn't have much chance to get down there very often.

After getting oriented to the country, we started the task of training the South Vietnamese to fly combat missions in the A-1E. The protocol for these missions was very similar to the practice missions I'd flown for years in America and Japan, except that in Vietnam we'd often fly over hostile territory.[1]

The Vietnamese students spoke English, which facilitated communication. They were highly motivated and very intelligent, but something seemed to hold them back from learning as quickly as pilots do in the U.S. One of the problems was that it was difficult for the Vietnamese to work with American combat pilots. I learned this firsthand when my squadron commander approached me one day and asked if I'd help a young Vietnamese trainee who was doing well in the classroom but got kind of rattled when he flew. I said, "Sure," and made arrangements to meet with the student.

As I sat down to talk with him about the mission we'd fly, I asked if there was anything specific he needed help with. He

---

1. See appendix B, "Vietnam Flight Protocol," for a specific, step-by-step description of the procedures we followed on a typical combat mission.

hesitated, as if he wanted to say something but was afraid to. I pushed him a little harder. Finally, he blurted out, "You Americans shout too much! You holler at us, and it scares us."

I hadn't realized it until then, but the highly assertive American approach to training was very foreign to the Vietnamese culture. The Vietnamese are quiet and seldom raise their voices.

"I promise I won't talk to you unless you request help or something goes wrong where I feel I need to take control." He accepted this and agreed to my help.

So I let him go, and he flew a beautiful ride—he handled the airplane just fine. We went inside, and I told the boss he was worth keeping. That pleased both my boss and the student. After a few more rides together, he checked out on the aircraft and was cleared for active duty. After the check-ride, he approached me and invited me to come meet his family and have dinner with them. That was a very unusual invitation. The Vietnamese seldom socialized with the Americans because they viewed us as boisterous and vulgar. I was flattered at his invitation and said I'd be honored to accept.

"The only trouble with eating at my place is that the food sometimes makes Americans sick—it doesn't taste good to you, and the thought of it seems offensive."

The Vietnamese eat many different types of meats that we find unpalatable, including rats and dogs, and they eat all parts of the animal.

"I'll hang in there and try it," I said with a smile.

He was pleased by that. So I went into the village and met his wife and baby, and we had a good meal together, although

I was careful not to ask what I was eating. They were very humble people, in their early twenties, and it was a choice experience for me to be in their home.

Living in Bien Hoa put us on the edge of an area identified as War Zone D, where there was always the sound of distant gunfire and cannons. One night I was sitting in my hooch while the second movie of the evening was playing in the base assembly area when the Viet Cong opened a mortar attack on our airfield. The first mortar landed on the wing commander's trailer and blew it apart. Fortunately, he was in his mortar bunker and wasn't hurt. I should have immediately run to a mortar bunker, but I didn't take the attack as seriously as I should have. We heard the enemy firing all the time, and I had gotten used to the mortars going off. Then the second mortar shell landed right on our front porch with a huge thud. It splintered the wood of the landing but failed to blow up. I'd undoubtedly have been killed if it hadn't been a dud. It scared me so badly I didn't know what to do. I just rolled off the bed and pulled the bunk on top of me. The next shell was a live one that exploded by the foot of our building, and the blast sent debris flying everywhere around me. I was shaken to the bone but somehow escaped serious injury. Unfortunately, six maintenance people were killed by fragmentation on the runway that night because they didn't have anywhere to run, and more than 100 base personnel were wounded. It was a mess. After that I always headed for the bunker at the first sign of trouble.

In spite of our best efforts, our training assignment with the Vietnamese didn't last long. They simply didn't make the kind of progress the Air Force thought they were capable of, partly because of the difficulty of adjusting to American pilots and partly because it was simply too confusing to learn basic skills in the pressure of the combat zone. It wasn't that the Vietnamese weren't capable pilots—they had a squadron flying out of Pleiku that was easily as effective as an American squadron. The difference was, that squadron had been trained in the United States.

It was decided that the best way to train the Vietnamese pilots was to send them to flight schools in America where they could learn in a controlled environment away from the pressure of competing with combat flights. So our students headed off to America, relieving us of our training responsibilities. My associates and I were now free for reassignment to active combat flying. We transferred north to Pleiku, near the mountainous border with Cambodia, to take an active combat assignment.

CHAPTER NINE

AIR COMBAT MISSIONS

FROM OUR BASE IN PLEIKU WE were assigned to fly missions to the southeast at Cam Ranh Bay and Nha-Trang, to the east at Qui Nhon and Bong Son on the South China Sea, and to the north at Da Nang near the demilitarized zone. Our effective range of flight made it impractical to go as far as North Vietnam, but there was plenty of hostile activity in the surrounding area to keep us busy.

It was frightening to go into combat for the first time because everything was unfamiliar. I constantly feared that if I lost my radio or wingman I wouldn't be able to navigate effectively to find my way home, because the rice fields and jungle were all so similar in appearance, regardless of the direction you traveled. The uncertainty was intensified by the high humidity of the area, which created a persistent haze that limited visibility.

After a few missions, I started to become familiar with the railroads, trails, and highways in the area, which lessened my anxiety considerably. Also, after coming under enemy fire, I quickly learned how to minimize my exposure while maintaining the effectiveness of the attack. At the rate of more than twenty combat missions per month, it didn't take long to gain experience.

We always flew our missions with at least two aircraft—a leader and a wingman. If it was a mission without ordnance, both aircraft could take off simultaneously in a preassigned formation. With ordnance, each aircraft took off individually, separated by ten-second intervals. That allowed a troubled aircraft to alert those scheduled to follow to hold in position until the problem was resolved. We needed this procedure because a heavily loaded aircraft under full acceleration simply can't stop when it reaches takeoff velocity, so it's up to the person following to avoid a collision. On one occasion I was flying wing to the operations officer who was flying the lead. He accelerated down the field with a full load of ordnance, and as he lifted off and rotated, his gun-cover doors accidentally opened, which immediately killed his flying speed. He should have alerted me to what was happening, but he was too busy concentrating on the aircraft to give warning. I took off ten seconds after he did with a full load of ordnance, probably weighing 8,000 pounds, and I pushed the engine right to the firewall. By the time I saw he was in trouble, there was simply no way I could stop. He didn't clear far enough off the side of the runway to avoid a near hit, and I came up right under his wingtip. We probably missed each other by less than a few feet. With that much ordnance on the two aircraft, a collision would almost certainly have proved fatal to both of us. Once airborne, we got our bearings together, and he returned to base while another aircraft came up to join me.

Some of my earliest missions in Vietnam were in support of the 1st Air Cavalry Division stationed out of Phong Dien but positioned at An Khe, approximately fifty miles due east of Pleiku. The Air Cavalry was frontline soldiers out of the same tradition as the army of the 1800s, except that they used helicopters instead of horses to get around. Typically, they'd be called out on a search-and-destroy mission when enemy activity was reported in the area. Ten to fifteen helicopters would be dispatched into the infiltrated area, where they'd swoop in and set down briefly to disgorge the troops. If they were under hostile fire during the landing, the helicopter would actually hover a few feet above the ground while the soldiers jumped out and moved into the underbrush to deal with the enemy. Hovering permitted a faster getaway. Usually, these missions lasted into the nighttime, so the cavalry would set up a defensive perimeter around their position to provide 360 degrees of protection from an enemy incursion.

We had two aircraft permanently assigned to support the cavalry, and the majority of our alerts came at night when the battle scene was most confusing. It was difficult to maneuver in the dark because the high humidity obscured all distinction between the horizon and the ground. Our pilots struggled with vertigo and disorientation to the point that we sometimes wondered if we were flying upside down or right side up. The only recourse was to fly these missions on instruments. That was a real challenge when the distance between friend and foe was sometimes measured in yards and the battle scene required instantaneous adjustments to the plan of attack.

When we first arrived on station, we'd check in with the forward air controller (FAC), an officer who was orbiting the area in an observation aircraft and was responsible for the air battle. He was in constant communication with troops on the ground and did his best to give us the most recent intelligence about where to attack. In the pitch blackness of a moonless night, however, it was still tough to tell the precise moment to release the ordnance or initiate a strafing run. In the early battles we tried to identify the target by watching the fiery trajectory of mortar attacks, but it was difficult to know who was launching the mortars. We'd communicate with the troops on the ground, reporting where we saw the mortar take off, and they'd usually respond, "Hold a minute while I check it out." By the time they confirmed it was the enemy, it was often too late to do any good, since the Viet Cong would fire a mortar, then immediately clear the area and move to a new location. We were constantly at risk of firing on our own troops.

We finally developed a resolution to the problem after consulting with the troops on the ground. Once a week we'd fly out to An Khe during the day to hold discussions with the Air Cavalry. The constant question on the table was how to safely identify our troops so we could place our fire in the proper location. On one occasion the dialogue went something like this:

"Why don't you set up flares around your perimeter so we can see your location?"

"If we set up flares, it will give away our position to the VC."

"They already know your position—that's why they're firing on you in the first place. We're the ones who need to know!"

They didn't have an answer to that.

Finally, they consented to give it a try. The next night they scrambled us to An Khe, and as we reached the area, we radioed to have them set off the flares. A fiery ring of twelve flare pots appeared in the jungle, with our troops inside the ring. That meant if a mortar launched from within the circle, we'd ignore it. But if a mortar launched outside the ring, we'd head straight for the spot at maximum speed and launch an attack. That made a huge difference in our effectiveness. It also solved the problem of vertigo, since the flare pots provided the visual reference we needed.

Sometimes we'd be dispatched on a search-and-destroy mission along "Highway 19," a supply road leading from North Vietnam through the Chu Yang Sin mountain range on the border of South Vietnam and Cambodia. To avoid detection, the North Vietnamese traveled the road by night. Someone at Command decided that these convoys had to be stopped because they were getting a lot of supplies through to the Viet Cong. We started a series of staged missions to keep the heat up throughout the night. Two aircraft were dispatched at 20:00, relieved by two other aircraft at 24:00 (midnight), another two at 02:00, and so forth.

The work was frustrating because we could see the

headlights bobbing through the thick jungle canopy as we approached the area, but when we got within about fifteen miles, the lights would go out and we couldn't see anything. The truck drivers simply hid in the darkness. It didn't make sense to waste ammunition without a clear fix on a target, so on most occasions we'd simply fly the route without getting the chance to fire.

One night, though, my wingman and I were coming near the end of our 04:00 patrol when I suggested that he fly north for ten minutes while I flew south just in case we might see something. A few minutes later he came on the radio and said, "You'd better come up here. I think we've got something." I headed north just as the sky was making the transition to twilight. In the feeble light, we could vaguely make out the shapes of some vehicles that were part of a convoy the Marines had fired on the previous day. The Marines' activity had spread the convoy out along a passage on the mountain. When we caught them, they were crossing an "underwater bridge" (a piled rock footing just under the surface of the water that they could drive across).

This sighting looked pretty solid, so we called for help, and Control immediately dispatched additional aircraft to support us. It still wasn't quite light enough to make out the targets with any certainty, but when the twilight turned to dawn, the sun started to cast shadows where the trucks were. The trucks themselves were virtually invisible because the North Vietnamese had effectively camouflaged them with branches and leaves, but the shadows were unmistakable. This was just the opportunity we'd been aching for, and we immediately started to attack with everything we had. Before long another flight joined us, and enemy targets went up in flame all up and down the line. Occasionally we'd hit an ammunition truck, and then the fireworks were spectacular, with flames leaping more than 100 feet into the morning sky. Everybody was exhilarated, because this single action could save potentially hundreds of our soldiers' lives by denying the enemy the ammunition they needed to mount an attack.

It didn't take long to use up all our ordnance, so we switched to strafing runs from fifty feet above the ground, flying up and down the trail firing on anything that moved or appeared to be a truck. The 20-millimeter cannons on the A-1E were bore-sited to fire 1,000 yards out, with two guns firing on the left wing and two on the right so that their paths converged at 1,000 yards. Of course, the North Vietnamese were firing back, and more than one of our aircraft landed with bullet holes. But the A-1E was extremely resilient and could often continue to fly even with a direct hit on the engine.

When I was totally out of ammunition, I broke off and started for home, replaced by a good friend of mine named Pappy Hill. He was an excellent and highly experienced pilot, but as he came down to fire on a truck that was stalled on the brow of a hill, he somehow misjudged and flew into the ground. The force of the crash killed him on impact. Ground troops moved in to extract his body, but it was a sad event for all of us who had lost this friend.

Protocol required that when we arrived at the scene of an action, we first checked in with the forward air controller to detail available ordnance so he could determine the best plan of attack. In addition to the four 20-millimeter cannons mounted on the wings, the Skyraider has fourteen closed stations of ordnance to carry bombs. The reporting might go something like this: "I've got six napalms and three Willy Pete's." (Willy Pete's were white phosphorus, a sulfur-based incendiary that burned hotter and longer than napalm.) The choice of which ordnance to use depended on the nature of the mission and the number of aircraft to be deployed. It wasn't unusual to load one bird with hard steel bombs, another with napalm, and a third with white phosphorus. Hard metal bombs were used to destroy major infrastructure, such as bridges, roads, and railroads, while soft bombs carried napalm and phosphorus to ignite fires in buildings and above-ground structures. Most battle sites had multiple types of targets, including buildings, bridges, and areas that needed to be defoliated or burned, which is why we'd launch multiple types of bombs.

After the forward air controller determined the plan of attack, the flight leader lined up with the forward air controller, who came in right under the fighters to lead them into the target. Once everyone was in position, the forward air controller would say something like, "This is Hound Dog 3-4—I'm going to mark the target." He rolled in with his spotter airplane and shot a white phosphorus rocket into whatever structure or bridge was the target. Once the smoke was visible, he flew in close to see where he placed the rocket and gave a final instruction, like, "Hit on my smoke" or "Hit twenty meters short of my smoke." He then cleared the area, and we launched our attack.

I remember one particular sortie we flew out of Bien Hoa to a target near Long Binh where the Viet Cong had gained enough strength to take over the countryside. Our job was to destroy their barracks. In the morning we flew down with one aircraft carrying a load of hard bombs, and the other plane carried soft bombs. We launched our attack without incident and returned to base. That afternoon they asked two of us to fly a second mission into the area. Rather than go in with split ordnance again, I suggested that we could do a lot of damage if we carried strictly soft bombs to launch against the dwelling units. They accepted my suggestion, and we loaded each bird with fourteen racks of napalm[1] and headed south. When we got to the area, there were some F-100s working the target, and they asked us to hold for a few minutes until they finished their run. We held off and watched the air show as the F-100s dropped their bombs. They finished and broke off for home, and the forward air controller directed us into a part of the enemy camp where the buildings were clustered close together. This was obviously a lucrative target with lots of opportunities to cause damage, so I told my wingman, "We're going to drop one can at a time, but don't drop a can of napalm unless you can light up two buildings."

There's something of an art to skipping cans of napalm to cause maximum damage. You fly in at about fifty feet and drop the bomb just short of the target. The forward motion of the aircraft sends the bomb skipping into the first building. A

---

1. Napalm is a petroleum jelly created by mixing diesel fuel with soap chips. About an hour or so after mixing, the jellied gas starts coagulating to the consistency of Jell-O pudding, and when you drop the bomb, the highly flammable mixture sticks to the trees and foliage.

small detonator cap in the nose of the napalm canister ignites the jelly that sprays inside the structure when the bomb strikes, and the whole thing goes up in flames immediately. Because the buildings were in such close proximity, we actually succeeded in sending a canister through the front door of one building, skipping it out the back door and into the next building. The intensity of the heat was so great that adjoining structures often caught fire from the sparks and heat from the buildings we'd struck.

The attack was devastatingly effective. We spent more than an hour working the place over, and before we were done the sky was full of black smoke, chased up by flames reaching high into the sky. Before exiting the area, we spied some armored sampans on the water next to the camp trying to make an escape, so we opened fire with our 20-millimeter cannons and sank three of them before they could get out into the river. Then we headed home.

As part of the assessment of our mission, one of the forward air controllers counted the buildings destroyed and said, "I've got to do this again—I can't believe it." His second count confirmed the first—104 buildings destroyed by two A-1E's—a new record—plus three military boats.

One of the more controversial aspects of the war was use of a defoliant called Agent Orange. It's actually similar to the herbicide Round-Up, but at industrial strength. It was delivered in bright orange barrels, which is why it received the nickname Agent Orange. The forest is so thick in Vietnam that it became nearly impossible to see the roads and trails from the air. The younger trees formed a lower canopy at approximately 50 feet, and the fully matured trees made a second canopy at nearly 200 feet. That made it easy for the Viet Cong to bring supplies and troops right through the heart of the jungle without detection. So when enemy activity was detected in an area by ground observers, Air Control dispatched C-123 cargo birds loaded with Agent Orange to spray on the trees above the trail. Two or three days later, the leaves and trees turned brown and died, exposing the road to view. On a number of occasions, I flew support missions to protect the C-123s while they dropped their load.

Once when I was fairly new in combat, they deployed us to follow a group of B-52 bombers that were assigned to destroy an area called the "Iron Triangle." It was located in an area full of caves where the Viet Cong tunneled in to store supplies and hide out during the day. The B-52s dropped hard bombs to crack open the entrances to the caves, and then we followed with napalm canisters that we skipped into the caves to burn the supplies stored there. Occasionally we'd see the napalm burn for a few minutes, and then there'd be a spectacular explosion that sent debris and smoke flying out the mouth of the cave, indicating a hit on an ammunition dump that exploded from the heat of the napalm.

Flying combat missions created some interesting emotions. In the hours leading up to a mission, we had idle time to think about what was coming, and at least some of the pilots stewed that this might be their day to get hit. Then we'd go through the familiar routine of briefing, suiting up, checking out the aircraft, and taking off. Depending on the day, we might make a clean drop of our load and make it home in time for lunch. On other days, particularly when providing ground support, we could be out for eight hours at a time, under constant enemy fire. Then it was back to the base and boredom. In any given twenty-four hour period, it was easy to go from anxiety to frenetic action to nothing to do, and finally to a tortured sleep in the jungle heat.

To relax, the guys played card games, watched movies, or attempted to play some physical games if the heat permitted. I brought a tennis racket, thinking it would be a good diversion, but the first time a friend and I walked down to the tennis court, we were wringing wet from the heat and humidity. The sun was so hot and miserable we played only about ten minutes before calling it quits. Physical exertion was very difficult in the heat.

One of the things I really loved about Vietnam was the tropical vegetation. There were banana trees, bamboo, palms, ferns and hundreds of varieties of fragrant flowers. Once in a while we'd leave the base and go shopping downtown. One of the items available was an excellent bicycle made in France. A good bicycle that would sell for $90 to $100 in America would run about $15 in Vietnam. So during free time, we'd hop on a bike and peddle into town. Vendors displayed their wares on the street corners, and some would squeeze fresh pineapples, mangoes, and other tropical fruit and serve the juice for about a penny a glass. I liked the taste but wondered about the hygiene of the vendors. Most of the men in Vietnam had the center top row of their teeth pulled as a sign of manliness, and they'd often chew betel nuts to deaden the area. It's a natural plant that has an effect similar to Novocain. The red juice of the betel nut looked like blood as it dripped from their mouths and onto their hands, which looked rather gruesome. On one trip into town I watched one of the locals drink from a glass, and when the next person stepped up, the vendor casually rinsed it in a tub of cold water and served the next customer with the same glass. After that I brought my own glass and straw from the commissary when I wanted fresh juice.

Another diversion in our off-time was listening to music. Stereo systems were very inexpensive, including popular Japanese brands like Sony and Akai. So we'd sit around and listen to music and check out tapes. Katrina Valenti was popular at the time, and there were several western artists that I liked, including Marty Robbins and Johnny Horton. Some of the younger men liked hard rock. Cameras were also a great buy, and a high-quality Nikon might cost us $15 to $20, while in the States they'd sell for $200 to $300.

Before long the missions started to add up. One day I had an assignment that somehow struck a nerve. There was a herd of cattle that had been stolen by the Viet Cong and taken into the hills to graze. Ground intelligence reported that they were butchering them for food. I was returning from a mission with some unused ordnance, and Control asked if I would mind hitting those cattle. I thought it was no big deal, so I reported that I'd be glad to. They gave me the vector, and I found the cattle quite easily. There was no ground fire to interfere, so I made a couple of passes firing my 20-millimeter cannons. I figured I'd come in at the end and release the ordnance to finish the job. When I flew over the scene it made me physically sick to my stomach—dead cows and wounded cows everywhere. Being a farm kid, I thought it was terrible to shoot animals like that, and I told them I'd rather not do that again. I denied food and comfort to the enemy, which was a legitimate target, but it brought out all the emotion I felt about being at war. War is a gruesome and cruel venture that forces men to kill. What a horrible waste.

Alcohol was readily available at the base, and after a hard day of flying, a lot of the pilots tried to relax at the Officers' Club with a few drinks. I'd join in their conversations but didn't drink alcoholic beverages. I've always liked the taste of lemonade, so I'd ask for a couple of lemons as I went through the chow line and then squeeze them later while relaxing with my buddies. Other people started picking up on it, which bothered the club manager, so he added lemonade as one of the beverages he served.

I know there's an image of prevalent drug use in Vietnam, but I didn't see it among the pilots I associated with. These were all professional, college-educated men who had volunteered for service in the Air Force. Most of them had families at home, and they didn't want to increase the risk of combat by taking drugs or narcotics that might not wear off in time for an air battle. But they did like alcohol.

One day Denny Hague, a good friend of mine said, "We've got to do something different than fly a mission, come home, drink booze, and go to sleep—only to get up the next morning and do it all over again."

I suggested that we go some place and relax a little bit. The guys liked that idea, so I called a friend of mine, Jump Myers, who was the detachment commander at Qui Nhon, near the ocean, and asked him about the chance of catching a flight to Clark Field in the Philippines.

He said, "Sure, there's a medical evacuation airplane going out of here all the time, and I think we can get you on one—come on over!"

So we got the day off, and five of us headed for Qui Nhon. The problem was finding a flight. A C-130 medical evacuation plane came in with a lot of wounded, and I asked if we could get on board. Jump said we'd have to get permission from the nurse. At first she was reluctant, since there were so many wounded, but eventually she took pity and told us it was okay if the pilot agreed. We told him what we wanted, and he said, "Sure, we'll take you. There's still some room on the back door—you can sit there."

We made the hop to the Philippines, and it was so good to eat fresh lettuce again. The food was great, the lemonade perfect, and we had a good, relaxing time completely away from the sound and fury of combat.

We stayed over that night and then had to think of some way to get back. We were already out on a limb, being that far from our home base, so I went down to Base Operations looking for airplanes that might be going in the direction of Pleiku. A Marine C-130 pilot came in and told the operations officer that he was going to Pleiku.

"That's just where we want to go," I said.

The pilot responded, "There's a C-141 that blew some tires while landing at Pleiku, and we need to get some replacements in. But I've heard it's pretty rough getting in there because of enemy fire and difficult ground conditions."

"Might be, but not when you're used to flying in and out of it every single day. We'd be glad to help you if you'll give us a ride."

He was relieved, and so was I. I called the club, and the guys came down immediately and put our names on the manifest. As we reached the final checkpoint, though, a master sergeant looked at the flight and said, "You can't go on this flight. There's live ordnance on board."

We laughed at that. "We fly with live ordnance every day. That's no problem"

"I don't care. The rules say you can't fly, so find another flight."

There were no other flights out, and we had to get back to Pleiku. I didn't know what to do. Then the Marine major who wanted us to fly with him asked the master sergeant, "What do we have to do for these men to fly on this airplane?"

"They'd have to be members of the crew."

So the major turned to me and said, "This is a pretty dangerous flight—we need three pilots. You're number three."

Then he said to one of the other guys, "You're the second gunner," and so forth until we all had assignments.

With that, the sergeant shook his head and let us pass. We made it past the remaining security checks and onto the airplane. At the end of the flight I told the major, "Sir, I'm awfully proud to have served with the United States Marines." He grinned and gave me a crisp Marine salute.

CHAPTER TEN

FLAMING ARROWS AND RESCUE MISSIONS

PROBABLY THE MOST DANGEROUS missions I flew were in support of a rescue effort. But they are also the most satisfying when successful.

Normal protocol required permission from the Vietnamese provincial chief, a position similar to that of the governor of a state, before we could launch a strike. The chiefs were very efficient in acting on our requests, but in emergencies there wasn't enough time to go through usual channels. To provide needed flexibility, a procedure was implemented so that if an American was in imminent danger, our controllers could launch a "Flaming Arrow," an immediate scramble, without waiting for permission from the Vietnamese.

The problem with rescue missions is that the enemy was always aware of our position and could focus their fire during those moments when the rescue team and support aircraft were most vulnerable. On one occasion a distress call was received from a fellow on the ground who had been shot twice while trying to drag some of his Army buddies to safety. They were lying in a ditch with the Viet Cong closing in on their position. Ground control launched a Flaming Arrow and dispatched those of us on alert to the scene. We connected with him by radio, but he was very emotional and difficult to communicate with. I told him the ordnance we had and offered to hit the Viet Cong, but he responded frantically, "You can't drop those because we're too close together. We're right among the enemy, and if you drop on them you'll hit us too!"

"Let's see if we can't work something out here," I started to reply, but he interrupted that I couldn't drop anything.

That was an irrational response—without support the Viet Cong would overrun their position in a matter of minutes, and they couldn't possibly defend themselves with so many wounded. They needed us, but I didn't know how to get him to calm down enough to let us help.

Just then a forward air controller came over the area in a helicopter and broke into the conversation. "You men on the ground, this is call-sign such and such, and we've got some A-1s up here that are going to get you out of there, so just stay quiet and let them do their job. You don't talk unless you have to! Is that understood?"

Given their desperate situation, it's easy to understand why the soldiers were scared, but having a major talk to them like that seemed to quiet them down.

I then said to the forward air controller, "Why don't you

have him throw up a smoke grenade, and I'll make a dry run over their position without dropping any ordnance. I'll go right over the top or to the side, whichever he likes. If he trusts my flying, I'll drop hot with napalm as often as needed to keep the Viet Cong off them."

The man on the ground didn't like the idea of putting up smoke because that would give away their position to the enemy, but eventually the FAC persuaded him. The white smoke billowed up, and I flew directly over their position on a cold run, as promised. He decided it would be okay to make a live drop, so I lined up and released the napalm as I crossed their position. It hit the jungle and ignited a small inferno, but safely away from our guys. He put up some more smoke, and I made a second dry pass, followed by a hot run. I think I ended up making twelve passes altogether—six cold followed by six hot.

On the thirteenth approach, he hollered into the radio, "Hold it, hold it!" and I thought I must have hit them, even though I was pretty sure of my firing.

"What's the trouble?"

"No trouble—the Viet Cong are running!"

The relieved sound in his voice made it all worthwhile. The forward air controller asked if we'd stay in the area for a while to provide cover for the medical evacuation helicopters they were bringing in to pick up the wounded, so my wingman and I stayed until after dark to cover them.

Through experience gained in the field, our rescue support became much more organized over the course of the next few months. In the beginning they'd scramble just a couple of A-1E's and helicopters but eventually learned to send out six to ten aircraft at a time under the direction of an "on-scene commander" who made decisions about how the support effort should be executed.

Periodically they'd dispatch a group of pilots from Pleiku to fly into Udorn (now Udon Thani) in Thailand to support attacks against targets in North Vietnam. Because Udorn was the northernmost point where the United States had landing rights, it became a staging base for rescue operations. When a major strike was scheduled, Jolly Green Giants (the rescue helicopters) landed about ten miles from the scene of the anticipated attack to wait for casualties. They'd just sit there with everything shut down, listening on their radios. The A-1E's flew into Udorn the night before with long-range fuel tanks on the wings, then took off in time to arrive in the general vicinity of the strike, maybe ten to fifteen minutes before it was scheduled to go down. We'd avoid flying directly over the target so as not to give away our intentions, but we remained close enough to respond almost instantly if a pilot got in trouble. If the bombers were successful, with no hits or casualties, the various aircraft on the rescue team returned home to Pleiku.

In the event of casualties, a rescue action was required. One troubled mission involved a group of four F-105s that were dispatched under the direction of a Major Randall to take out a three-span bridge just southeast of Dien Bien Phu in North Vietnam. I was flying as wingman to Smokey Stover, who brought us to the area in time to witness the strike.

Major Randall was called the "Cadillac lead," and he instructed his pilots that he'd be the first bird to roll in and hit the target. He came around the turn and rolled in with hard bombs, hitting the bridge with enough force to destroy it on the first pass. But the North Vietnamese hit him with ground fire when he pulled up, forcing him to eject from the airplane. The parachute opened successfully, and he landed by a large tree some ten miles east of Dien Bien Phu.

Now it was our job to take over the scene and get him out of there. Smokey called back to the helicopter crew waiting on the ground, and they cranked up and headed toward our position.

Smokey remained on station to cover Major Randall while I broke off and went out to find the helicopter and direct them to the rescue site. When we connected, I radioed the helicopter pilot that when we approached the rescue area, I'd accelerate the A-1E, push over, make a low pass directly over the tree that Randall was under, pull up, and come back and support the helicopter crew in the pick-up. When the time arrived, I made the maneuver as planned, but the helicopter failed to locate the downed pilot. His green camouflage fatigues simply blended in with the jungle. The scene was very dangerous, and the helicopter picked up some ground fire on the first pass. I led them in for a second pass, but they failed to spot him on that attempt as well. This time the helicopter came under heavy fire. The pilot said they'd suffered some damage to the engine and would have to break off if we couldn't get him out of there fast. I contacted Major Randall and told him he had to do something quick to make himself visible to the chopper. He scrambled for a few moments, looking for something, and then said triumphantly, "I have my Mae West—I'll inflate that and step out from the tree." A Mae West is a fluorescent colored life preserver for staying afloat in water, and he stood out like a bright green thumb in the jungle when he pulled the canister to inflate it. It was beautiful. The helicopter crew spotted him immediately and flew over to his position. They attempted to drop the penetrator (a hook to winch the downed pilot up into the aircraft), but it had been damaged by the ground fire. The helicopter pilot took a great risk and settled down right to the top of the trees so the crew could lower a rope. At that point they were sitting ducks for enemy fire. Major Randall tied the rope under his arms, and the helicopter crew pulled him up and took off for home. We flew along and escorted them out of the area.

Throughout the ordeal, the major's wingmen had relentlessly circled the area, calling us and saying, "Where do you want us to strike?"

Smokey always replied, "We want to keep it as quiet as we can down here."

The F-105 crews had refused to abandon their leader, so they'd kept circling the area, waiting for an opportunity to attack any North Vietnamese who might try to take their guy out.

Back at base, Smokey and I went over to check on the major's condition. Rather than be grateful for our help, he was really angry and accused us of firing at him while he was on the ground. We assured him that we'd been firing at the North Vietnamese behind him and that only the shell casings of our expended ammunition had fallen on him. It took some convincing before he accepted that we were some of the good guys.

The Air Force recognized our efforts by awarding Smoky Stover and me the Distinguished Flying Cross for meritorious service under severe combat conditions. We'd taken quite a number of hits from enemy fire while directing the rescue helicopter into position and providing support cover during the rescue.

I had a close call returning to Pleiku after another mission. We'd flown to the north and were scouting out one of the roads on our return trip. Rather than simply waste fuel getting home, we'd use the return trip as a reconnaissance opportunity to provide current information on enemy troop movements to Air Force Intelligence. The usual method was for one pilot to fly high for communications, the other close to the ground to check out the road. I was down in the low slot as we came around a bend in the river. I took a pretty solid hit from enemy fire. My wingman, 1,000 feet overhead, called me and said, "Did you just get hit?"

"Pretty hard, in fact!"

"Thought so—some dust or debris fell off your plane in a small cloud, so I figured something must have hit you. Are you okay?"

I checked the instruments, and all systems were operating normally. "I'm okay—let's circle around and see where they're hiding."

I assumed there was an enemy gun placement somewhere on the mountain next to the river, so I circled and came around. Sure enough, there was a cave on the side of the mountain that had four machine guns in front of it, mounted on a track so they could roll the nest back into the mountain for protection after firing on an unsuspecting aircraft. We reported this to the controllers and requested permission to fire our remaining ordnance. Permission was granted, and I rolled out and skipped my bombs right into the mouth of the cave. I don't know how much damage I caused, because those guns fired the next time we came by on a later mission. That really infuriated me, so whenever I heard about F-105s that were returning with unused ordnance, I'd ask permission to have them fire on that cave again. Most were happy to oblige. Before I transferred out of the area, I think we destroyed half the mountain trying to get at the guns in that cave.

One of my friends got killed in an unfortunate accident while flying a support mission. The infantry located a Viet Cong training camp located on the banks of the Mekong River and requested air support to knock it out. He flew in low over the river, and just as he approached the camp, he pickled (released) his napalm cans right into the heart of the camp, then pulled up sharply to miss the detonation. What he didn't see, until too late, was a dead tree sticking up in his flight pattern. He couldn't gain altitude fast enough to miss hitting it, and a six-inch branch tore into the belly of his aircraft. The impact threw him into an unplanned roll, and he crashed into the trees.

I had a similar experience coming across a river, probably fifty feet above the water, and was just about to release a bomb on the other side when suddenly there was a tree sticking right up in my path. Acting on pure instinct, I pulled the airplane up immediately so that it practically stood on its tail, and I just missed hitting the tree. All this happened while I had my finger on the trigger to launch a napalm canister, and for some reason I thought if I just rotated the airplane in a quick roll I could still release the napalm and hit the target. So I rolled and pickled the can. I felt it leave the aircraft, but there was nothing but silence. The forward air controller came on the radio: "Did you drop?"

"Yes, I did, and I saw the bomb go—but I don't know where it is now."

"Well, I can't see it down here."

Suddenly a brilliant flash appeared way up on the side of mountain.

"I think you delayed dropping too long."

"I think I dropped at the right time, but I was pulling up to miss a tree, and it must have carried the bomb with me a little bit."

"Well, if that's the case, you tossed it about two miles!"

I guess that shows how much the angle of release affects the placement of a bomb!

The canister didn't do any damage, but that dead tree about scared me to death. When you're pickling soft bombs, you have to fly in close to the ground, with trees all around, and I'd trained myself to look for the green canopy. But I hadn't thought about dead trees. From that point forward, I was religious in looking for anything that might be in my flight path.

Some of the weapons developed for ground support had a terrifying impact on the enemy. We were sitting on alert at Pleiku when a call came to help out an infantry unit of the First Air Cavalry, some of the most effective soldiers to serve in Vietnam. The unit was moving in on a concentration of enemy soldiers, using the jungle as cover to hide their approach. We took off and checked in with the forward air controller flying in a small spotter aircraft.

"You've got about six minutes to help," he said, "and then the unit will move past this position. Our forces have backed a contingent of enemy combatants into the jungle at these coordinates, so drop some ordnance on the bad guys!"

My wingman was flying with napalm and white phosphorus, and I was carrying a group of fragment clusters, which are small, 120-pound bombs that make a small sound when they hit (not at all like the big 500-pound bombs used to destroy infrastructure). But the fragment clusters are wrapped in a steel casing that turns into shrapnel when the bomb explodes, and it just tears through people.

We made an initial pass and launched our weapons against the North Vietnamese, apparently with devastating effect, because the guys on the ground told us we could break off the attack. The North Vietnamese resistance had evaporated.

The next morning I sat next to an Army major at our regular briefing. He leaned over and mentioned that he was with the Big Red unit in the field that had been supported the day before, and he wanted to come in and personally thank us for helping them out. He seemed quite emotional about it. When the briefing was over, everyone got up and went their own way, and I lost track of the Major. I went over to Jump Myers, the detachment commander, and asked who that fellow was.

"I don't know," he said. "I thought he was your friend."

Apparently the major didn't know any of us; he just wanted to come in and say thanks and then took off. That happened quite frequently. We'd meet people, especially on Fridays when we'd go out in the field to talk with the cavalry face-to-face to try to figure out how to help them better. Those meetings were extremely productive. It was there that we decided on using smoke grenades as markers so we could tell where friendly forces were, as mentioned earlier. Then, once the Viet Cong began using their own smoke grenades to confuse us, it was suggested that our guys use different-colored smoke (yellow, green, red, or blue) so we could distinguish them from the enemy.

Even though I'd been in Vietnam for only six months by this point, it felt like an eternity. I had more than 150 missions under my belt, and the stress was high. Before my term was over, the casualty rate for pilots with whom I'd arrived in Vietnam was around 40 percent. George McKnight and George Bolstead were shot down and taken prisoner. Another got hit in the Tonkin Gulf by a big gun, but he made it out. He had an interesting story. He told us that the manual said that if you get hit over water, you can skip the belly of your airplane on the water and kind of hydrofoil across the surface. He tried that when he got hit, but instead of skidding across the surface like it was supposed to, the aircraft just dove straight down into the water. "It doesn't float like the book says it does," he said sardonically. Two other pilots in our group were flying out of Qui Nhon, and the mountains were too high for the heavy load on the airplane. They crashed into the side of a hill and were killed. It was always disheartening to lose a friend like that.

I was pretty homesick and wanted a chance to go home. Realla and I had promised each other we'd write a letter every single day, and we honored that commitment. However, the post office wasn't entirely predictable in how letters would arrive. Sometimes a letter mailed on Friday would get there before one mailed on the preceding Tuesday or Wednesday. That happened once when Realla wrote that one of the boys had twisted his toe, injuring it severely. She mailed that letter and then a couple of days later wrote to tell me that it looked like his foot was all right. I got the second letter first, which made me kind of crazy wondering what had happened to his foot in the first place. The good part of the mail service, though, was that it was free to servicemen, and the letters always got through in the end.

One day I received word that our youngest boy needed surgery to remove his tonsils, and I capitalized on that as a chance to request an emergency leave. It was pretty tough to get a leave without some kind of compelling reason, such as a medical problem, so I went to my commanding officer and told him that I really should be there with the kids while Realla nursed this one. He agreed and cut some orders giving me a leave home. I caught the first available transport and made it home to Kuna a couple of days after that. What a joyful experience to see my wife and boys again. It was so quiet and peaceful out on the farm, without the constant drone of military aircraft and equipment, or the incessant sound of battle. It was also cool and dry compared to Vietnam, and in some ways I wanted to stay there forever. But that wasn't an option, so when the leave came to an end, I reluctantly told everyone good-bye. I think I dreaded getting back on an airplane but knew I had to go. The trip home was just a short time after the rescue of Major Randall at

Dien Bien Phu, in which I'd been awarded the Distinguished Flying Cross, and I'm not sure Realla was impressed. She said something like, "Now don't go being a hero; we want you to come home!" I kissed her good-bye and trudged up the stairs and onto the airplane that would take me back to Vietnam.

CHAPTER ELEVEN

THE SILVER STAR MISSION

It didn't take long to fall back into the routine of flying. The North Vietnamese regulars had succeeded in advancing some serious incursions into the mountainous area just south of the demilitarized zone that separated North and South Vietnam, and the Allies were hard pressed to contain them. Most of the action was taking place approximately 150 miles north of Pleiku and 50 miles west of Da Nang (our alternate air base). It was treacherous territory to fly into, with narrow mountain valleys that crossed into one another in a confusing maze. At less than thirty miles from the ocean, the valleys often filled with fog and clouds, making it extremely difficult to find an entrance to the valleys where ground troops needed support. To get below the clouds and fly a strafing run, we had to come in at about fifty feet. With foothills and mountains reaching elevations of nearly 7,000 feet, any false turn could prove fatal.

The valleys also provided a remarkable advantage for the North Vietnamese anti-aircraft batteries, as they could mount guns on the side of the hills to fire down on us rather than up. It's much easier for a gun crew to sight a weapon to fire vertically or depressed on a target that has to follow a precise angle of approach. Compared to hostile ground-fire in the lowlands, this was murderous. Our aircraft came back with holes in the fuselage on nearly every flight.

On March 4 or 5, 1966, intelligence reported that the North Vietnamese were planning a major assault on a Special Forces position in a remote location known as the Ashau Valley. The valley is six miles long and just one mile wide. Approximately 450 of our men occupied an old French fort to guard the approaches from North Vietnam, and they'd managed to capture some North Vietnamese scouts who were very candid in telling them what to expect in the next few days. More than 2,000 North Vietnamese regulars were moving into position near the valley to trap the Special Forces and were already in the process of setting up machine-gun nests and anti-aircraft batteries in the foothills. Even though they were the best soldiers America had, the Special Forces were badly outnumbered, and they had a rough time of it right from the beginning when the battle started on March 6.

On the morning of March 9, I'd just finished flying a mission and was getting set to fly another in the afternoon when we got word that we were to scrap the assigned mission because a fight was on at Ashau and they needed our help. I said okay and changed our flight plan. Apparently an AC-47 had been scrambled out of Da Nang to provide covering fire for the ground forces using three "Puff the Magic Dragon" mini-guns. These guns are terrible weapons, firing 6,000 rounds per minute (100 per second), which is so fast that when they're firing, all you see is a sheet of flame tearing out from the side of the aircraft with a blue haze of smoke rising from the nozzles. Hence the nickname. It actually sounds like one continuous explosion because the individual concussions come too quickly for the ear to distinguish one from the other.

The AC-47 made an initial strafing run down the "tube" at Ashau. On its next pass, the North Vietnamese hit its left engine. As the pilot banked starboard to exit the area, he lost his right engine but somehow managed to make an emergency landing and get off a "Mayday" call for help. A rescue was ordered for the crew of the AC-47, and we were diverted to provide additional support for the infantry in the fort in place of the AC-47.

Bruce Wallace was my wingman that day as we took off from Pleiku and headed northwest. The weather was extremely poor, with an expected ceiling of just 300 feet in the valley. At approximately seventy-five miles out, we hit a cloud bank that made it obvious the weather was not going to cooperate, so we slid out to the west where it wasn't quite so cloudy. As we reached the general area, I started probing the canyons to figure out where the Special Forces camp was, but with no success. On my third attempt, I came up out of the clouds and crossed within a few yards of the nose of a helicopter, which about scared me (and the pilot of the helicopter) to death. We recovered from the near miss, and I raised him on my radio.

"Do you know where Ashau is?"

"We just came out of there—picked up some of the dead and wounded from the AC-47."

"Can you direct me in?"

"Just keep going and you'll come to a saddle in the mountains. Go over the saddle and drop down into the little valley on the other side. When you see the smoke and start getting shot at, you'll know you're in the right place."

We proceeded as directed, and when we reached the area, I checked in with the airborne command post to see what they wanted us to do. They connected us to the troops on the ground, who reported, "We're being overrun and are consolidating into the northwest mortar bunker. The fort is shaped like a triangle, with a mortar bunker at each point. You can hit anything that moves on the southern wall."

The situation was extremely desperate, because the North Vietnamese knew that if the cloud covering lifted, we'd wipe them out. They stood to lose more than 2,000 troops. So the last thing they were going to do was waste time and effort to take prisoners. It was a life-and-death struggle.

"What do you want us to do first?"

"Take out the AC-47. The guns are still hot, and if the North Vietnamese get hold of them, they'll turn them on us!"

That was a pretty dangerous request. Both Bruce and I were loaded with hard bombs, which typically required a dive-bomb approach to release. Usually, when you dive bomb, you start your run at 5,000 feet above the deck and roll in at about a 45-degree dive to the ground, releasing the ordnance at 2,500 feet so you won't be hit by your own blast. The fragmentation can flip up and hit you.

But with a ceiling at 300 feet, we'd have to skip the hard bombs in. It was an extremely difficult maneuver, with an almost certain chance of getting hit ourselves by fragments thrown up from the deck by the force of the blast. As the on-scene commander, I made the decision that Bruce was best suited to pull it off, so I told him to get the AC-47. He simply said, "Okay," and headed off down the canyon to gain some room to maneuver. When he was probably two or three miles back, he executed a 180-degree turn and came back with all the speed he could get out of the old airplane. Staying just under the cloud ceiling so he could get a clear shot, he released all six bombs simultaneously, then pulled the nose almost straight up, rocketing up through the clouds and breaking out on top. It was amazing flying, one of the best maneuvers I've ever seen, and he managed to get up without getting hit. The AC-47 wasn't so lucky, and it went up in a tremendous fireball that completely obliterated any hopes the North Vietnamese may have had of capturing it.

By this time Air Command had brought in additional aircraft to help us keep the North Vietnamese off the Special Forces. Since Bruce and I were the ones who knew the lay of the land, it now became our responsibility to guide them in for the attack.

I left Bruce up on top to circle the area and collect the aircraft, while I stayed down underneath to fire on the North Vietnamese and direct the attack when the supporting aircraft got under the ceiling. From where Bruce was, he could see the mountain peaks, so he could stay oriented to where the approach was, and he just orbited in a circle while other aircraft fell into formation behind him. When they were ready, he'd line up an approach and bring them down through the clouds. By following him directly, they would come down through the clouds and miss the mountain peaks. We put quite a few airplanes in that way. Eventually, heavier clouds moved in, and we lost the needed reference point to bring in additional planes.

After about three and a half hours, Bruce called in that he was "Bingo" (running low on fuel), so we requested permission to return to base. Just about that time two C-123 cargo planes checked in with medical supplies and ammunition. With no prior knowledge of the area, it was impossible for them to find their way in to make a drop. The command post asked if we could stay and help them. I suggested that instead of returning to Pleiku, we could fly to Da Nang, which was just twenty minutes flying time away. That would give us a few extra minutes to help the big planes find their way in. Clouds had now obscured all approaches from above, and Bruce had no way to find his way in. I was still flying underneath the ceiling, looking for light spots in the clouds that might indicate a possible approach. When you're looking down on clouds, it's all darkness. But looking up through the clouds, you can see light spots where the clouds are starting to thin enough that a pilot could descend and have enough visibility to make a decent approach to the fort. Eventually I found a promising hole, and I checked in with Bruce:

"I think I've found a hole. Why don't you get the 123s

lined up, and I'll fly straight up through the hole where you can see me. Then I'll twist around and head straight back down through the same spot. You follow me with the 123s in trail, and we'll get them on a good approach to the fort."

"Roger, we'll be waiting."

Well, it worked beautifully. I shot straight up through the hole, and when I reached clear sky, I twisted into a roll at the top and headed straight back down where I'd come from. It was a lot like pushing a needle up and out of the fabric, then back down to complete the stitch.

When I reached the ceiling, I leveled out on a perfect angle for the approach, and Bruce and the C-123s came after me. The ceiling was so low they had to drop the supplies from fifty feet, which didn't give a parachute much room to slow down the fall.

On the first pass through, the bundles released successfully, and the C-123s flew down the canyon and back up into the clear, where they made a 180-degree turn and came back for the next approach. We used the same technique where I flew up to thread the needle and then flew back down through the hole. The pilots in the C-123s did a great job and landed fourteen bundles in the six or seven passes that we orchestrated. When the last bundle was dropped, Bruce indicated that he was now "Bingo" for Da Nang, which meant he had to get out of there fast or he'd run out of fuel. I was in about the same condition, so I sent him off and finished getting the 123s out of the area and requested permission to return to base to refuel.

That's when two B-57s checked in. They'd arrived at the scene to bomb the outskirts of the camp. I was listening on their frequency when they checked in, and I told them the cover was too low for them to drop hard bombs at the speeds they had to fly. They'd blow themselves out of the sky!

"We're not carrying hard bombs—we have wing-to-wing napalm cans that we want to skip in at fifty feet. Can you get us pointed in the right direction?"

I said yes, even though I thought it was risky for a jet to launch napalm. My fuel situation was really quite desperate, but it seemed a huge waste for those big aircraft to lose out on the opportunity of providing such desperately needed support to the ground troops, so I stayed in the area long enough to get them down through the clouds and on a good approach. As soon as I could, I raced up and out of the clouds to head for my alternate base.

When I reached the Da Nang area I checked in with GCA radar (ground control), and they gave me a precision approach into the field at Da Nang. I looked at my fuel gauge and told them I didn't have enough fuel to run the standard square box pattern where the radar gives you the vectors for landing. "You just bring me over Da Nang and I'll run my own pattern," I said.

When I broke out of the clouds and into the clear, I was at about 800 feet and right over the airfield. I contacted the tower for permission to land while dropping my gear and flaps for a final approach.

"You are number two in the emergency pattern."

Number two? I thought incredulously. I radioed back that I couldn't wait.

"A C-123 is on final approach with a fire onboard, and

he's experienced a number of explosions in primary systems. He's number one, and you're number two."

I rolled back up and looked down, and I could see him on final approach. He was just a little bit beyond me, so I said, "I'll take the runway, the taxi way, or the grass in between, but I can't go around."

I went ahead and landed on the runway. That forced the C-123 pilot to land on the taxi way, which he did without any problem. Still, I got criticized for it. My only choice, really, was to bail out and let the aircraft crash or land as I did.

I caught up with the pilot of the 123 later and apologized, and he was fine with what had happened.

That was a heck of a day. Bruce and I made arrangements to get the airplanes fueled up, ran down to the officer's club to get a sandwich or two, and then headed back to the flight line. Our aircraft were fueled up and ready to go, so we headed back to Pleiku, arriving at the base at 22:00.

Although I didn't learn about it until later, both Bruce and I were nominated for medals. I was awarded the Silver Star for my role as on-scene commander, and Bruce received the Distinguished Flying Cross.

CHAPTER TWELVE

THE RESCUE AT ASHAU VALLEY

WE WENT TO BED EXHAUSTED, hoping to get some sleep before our next mission. Unfortunately, the situation on the battlefield was getting desperate, and at 04:00 we got an unexpected wakeup call. There was hostile action all up and down the line, and they needed as many planes in the air as they could muster. So we headed for a briefing at sunrise. My wingman, Paco Vazquez, didn't have too many missions under his belt and was fairly new at flying this type of close support, but he was a good, thoughtful pilot who kept his wits about him. We scrambled and headed on a vector to support the Big Red division. Just as I was about to check in with Air Control at Kontum, we got a call on "Guard," the emergency radio frequency.

"Take your birds to these assigned coordinates. There's a fight up there and they need some immediate help."

"Is that Ashau?" I asked.

"That's confirmed. The camp's been overrun, but some of the men made it through the night and are still holding on."

We changed course and headed north, ascending to 12,000 feet to get above the clouds and into the Ashau Valley area. There were a lot of airplanes that had been diverted there because of the emergency, including some from as far away as Qui Nhon. I checked in with the forward air controller and was assigned to join two other birds circling at 8,000 feet (the mountain peaks were 7,000 feet). He had another flight at 9,000 feet and a third at 10,000 feet. There were jet aircraft, A-1s and C-123s, to name a few. He stacked the aircraft in layers to have some control over them, breaking out particular groups as needed for bombing or other support.

The biggest problem when we arrived was that pilots were having trouble finding the camp through the clouds. The terrain was intimidating, and there was a lot of uncertainty about the location of the various peaks that weren't tall enough to poke through the cloud cover. Consequently, there wasn't a lot of support being provided to the men on the ground because it was so hard to find the way in.

One of the pilots circling at 9,000 feet suggested that some of us should head over toward Laos to see if we could find an approach from the west. I didn't know it at the time, because he used his call sign, but it was my friend Jump Myers from Qui Nhon. As the on-scene commander, I decided to accept his advice, so we took off in that direction. Partway there, I spotted a hole in the clouds in a location that seemed familiar from the previous day, so I radioed to Jump that I thought we could get into the valley that way. Jump and his wingman, Hubie King, joined Paco and me in a 180-degree turn to go back to the spot. Two other pilots, Denny Hague and Jon Lucas, checked in and joined our group. I instructed them to remain orbiting in case we needed them for backup. The valley was too restrictive to handle six aircraft at once. I checked the hole a second time to make sure we were above the valley floor and was reassured to see a plowed field down below. With that I said, "Tally-Ho," and went down first, with the other three following in trail. We couldn't fly side-by-side because the mountains were too close.

We got down below the ceiling and had pretty good visibility. I found the landmarks I needed to orient myself to the approach and started heading in the direction of the old fort. While it helped our visibility to have the ceiling at 800 feet, it also meant it was easier for the big guns the enemy had mounted on the sides of the hill to fire down on us. As we reached the scene of the battlefield, it was like a dark nightmare. The black, acrid smoke rising in columns from the ground merged with the cloud ceiling and mixed with ash from the multiple fires created by repeated napalm strikes. Burned-out trees and wrecked vehicles lay haphazardly on the valley floor, and we could actually smell the cordite from the explosives.

I switched over to FM radio, flew right in on the deck, and buzzed the fort while contacting one of the Special Forces guys on the ground: "I'm the A-1 that just buzzed you—what can we do to help?"

"We've been overrun. There are about 180 of us left. They've got everybody else. We're crowded with the wounded in the corner of the northwest mortar bunker. Except for that, you can hit anywhere else in the camp you like."

With that I set up an attack on the south wall of the fort. We flew about two miles down the center of the valley with the North Vietnamese firing what appeared to be .50-caliber guns (.50-calibers have a red tracer rather than the green tracers used in other small weapons). That made the approach very challenging. On our first run Hubie King, Jump Myers's wingman, got hit in the Plexiglas canopy that encloses the cockpit, making it impossible for him to see through the smoke and wind that buffeted his face. He broke off and headed for the nearest field at Da Nang.

Normally, you'd first set up a run to drop bombs to reduce the danger of blowing up if you got hit, but I could see the North Vietnamese swarming toward the Special Forces, so I decided to do a strafing run first. I set up an attack pattern where I flew in with four cannon firing directly in front of our forces. Paco slid over thirty feet and made a second pass, followed by Jump Myers, who followed thirty feet to the right of Paco. The object was to drive the Vietnamese back from our people and into the jungle. The first pass got them moving; the second and third caught and killed many of them and drove the rest away from our men. At the end of the run, we circled up and to the left to set up a repeat pattern to keep backing them toward the jungle. We must have been pretty effective, because Command later attributed between 300 and 500 enemy dead because of our strafing.

About the time Jump completed his second run, they hit him with something big in the engine, and he started to lose power. I could see him out ahead of me because I'd already entered the pattern for another run, and he was trailing fire all the way from the engine past the tail of his aircraft. I was relieved to hear his voice in my headset: "This is Surf 41. I've been hit, and hit hard."

I responded immediately, "Hobo 51—Rog, you're on fire and burning clear back past your tail!"[1]

"Surf 41—Rog, I'll have to put her down on the strip."[2]

Even though Jump had a parachute on, it wouldn't do him any good since the aircraft didn't have an ejection seat, and he didn't have enough altitude for the chute to open. He pulled up a little but didn't have enough power to get very high. He reported later that he briefly thought of riding it into the jungle. While it was likely that the huge propeller on the A-1E would have cleared out some of the trees when it hit, the fire onboard the aircraft made it even more likely that there would have been an explosion when he crashed.

Jump opened the canopy to get rid of the smoke, but the fire crawled right up into the cockpit, so he closed the canopy and endured the smoke.

I reminded him that he had 6,000 pounds of bombs on board that he needed to get rid of before attempting to land.

---

1. Each squadron had its own call sign. I was assigned "Hobo," while one of our companion squadrons was "Surf." Rescue missions were identified as a "Sandy." The call sign reduced the risk of misunderstanding when communicating by radio.

2. Dialogue as quoted in T. R. Sturm, "Into the Valley of Death," *The Airman* (official magazine of the United States Air Force), March 1967, 5.

He pulled the emergency release, allowing the bombs to fall without exploding. Relieved of that burden, he gained enough altitude to make a 180-degree gliding turn to line up with the runway, just 200 feet below. The loss of power made it difficult for him to maneuver to avoid coming under fire from a number of heavy guns the enemy had positioned to the east of the runway.

With all the smoke in his canopy, he couldn't see very well, so I flew alongside to tell him what was happening and when to set down. He made a clean approach, but it looked like the runway was way too short to land on, so I told him to raise the gear to prevent the airplane from cartwheeling at the end of the runway. He pulled the gear up just as he touched down, and I watched it fold as he landed on his belly. The aircraft settled on the runway. He had tried to release the extra fuel tank attached to the belly prior to landing, but the release had failed, and the tank blew as soon as he touched ground. A huge billow of flame went up behind him, and the fuel made a path of fire that followed him as he skidded about 800 feet before stopping. At the end of his skid, the right wing must have caught the ground, because it spun him a bit, and he spilled off to the right side of the runway. The flame followed him down and caught up with him, and the A-1E exploded into a huge ball of orange fire. The explosion appeared so devastating I couldn't imagine how anyone could survive, but I circled the airfield just in case. After forty seconds with no movement, I reported that he probably wasn't going to make it. Suddenly Jump emerged from the cockpit. At just the right moment, the wind picked up and blew the flames away to the right side of the aircraft, clearing an escape path through the smoke. He ran across the wing and dropped into the field, where he raced for a muddy little ditch. In spite of enemy fire, he was able to slide into the ditch for cover and quickly covered his face and body in mud to camouflage himself as best he could.[3]

I contacted the command post, reporting that the downed pilot was alive and that we needed a rescue helicopter. The Marines were supporting us out of a base called Phu Bai, and they said the chopper would be there in about twenty minutes. We returned to our strikes—both to protect Jump and to provide cover for the south wall of the fort. I instructed Denny Hague and Jon Lucas to join us in the valley to add some firepower, since Paco and I had used up most of our ammunition. They came flying through the gauntlet, which Denny Hague described as being similar to flying into a large sports arena where everyone in the stands has guns that they're shooting at you.[4] After about ten minutes of circling and firing, I called the command post to ask where the chopper was, and they reported that it was still probably twenty minutes out. In other words, they were guessing and had no real idea how long it would take. Command asked if we'd come up out of the clouds and escort the rescue chopper back down when it arrived.

That wasn't an option. Jump's position was so precarious

---

3. The reason it took him so long to exit the aircraft was that when he found himself surrounded by flames, he decided to lighten his load by stripping off his parachute, gun, helmet, and survival gear before attempting to run to safety.

4. From a transcript of a video interview with Denny Hague by Nathan and Kelly Fisher. Used with permission.

that if any of us pulled out, the Vietnamese would immediately swarm in and kill him. Even with our covering fire, it was down to a matter of minutes before they'd overrun his position. I considered the state of affairs on the ground to determine the feasibility of going in for a landing, but it didn't look good. The physical condition of the runway was terrible, and it looked like it was too short to accommodate an A-1E anyway. I called Airborne Command and asked the length of the runway. They replied that it was 3,500 feet. A quick mental calculation showed that with the current wind conditions I might be able to land in 3,000 feet. Even in the best of conditions, however, it was almost suicidal to land an aircraft as large and slow as the A-1E while exposed to direct enemy fire. A helicopter crew can fire their weapons from the side doors to hold the enemy at bay while executing a rescue, but I'd be defenseless while sitting on the ground.

It made no logical sense, but I felt a strong impression that I should do this. Jump was one of the family—one of the fellows we flew with—and I couldn't stand by and watch him get murdered without at least trying to rescue him. I said a quick mental prayer, asking for help, and the feeling I received seemed to confirm that I should attempt a rescue. I reported my decision to Airborne Command, and they strongly discouraged it. I didn't want to go in, but I decided to go with my feelings in spite of their advice. So I backed off and came into the wind over the runway. Smoke coming out of the fort obscured my visibility as I dropped the gear and flaps. I entered the pattern on a good approach, but when the smoke thickened around me, I couldn't be sure; it would be disastrous to cut the power if I wasn't over the runway. So I held the power on until I broke out of the smoke, and sure enough, I was right over the runway. I cut the power and touched down.

When I hit, it was obvious that I couldn't stop the airplane. The makeshift runway was constructed out of pierced steel planking that was very slick on top. To add to the problem, the North Vietnamese had hit it with mortars in a number of places, tearing the planking into jagged steel shards that I'd have to maneuver around if I didn't want to blow out my tires. There were all kinds of other garbage on the runway. Metal barrels and fragments of tin roofs had been blown onto the runway from all the bombing, and somebody had dropped five or six rocket pods that I hit. In spite of my dodging and weaving, I couldn't get enough of a grip to land, so I powered up and bounced off the runway and decided to try to come in from the other direction. That was going to make for a very tough landing, because I wasn't flying into the wind, which helps you slow down. After making the turn, I touched right at the end of the plating and immediately stood on the brakes, skidding down the runway. The brakes began to fade from heat as I reached the 2,000-foot mark, and I realized that Control must have been wrong about the length of the runway (they'd actually misread the map, and the runway was just 2,500 feet). I was going to run out of runway, so I searched for the best place to go and saw some brown grass at the end that might support me. I went off the runway and over a little embankment that slowed me down a bit, and I slid into what turned out to be a fuel storage dump. There were a bunch of fifty-five-gallon fuel barrels in there that I couldn't avoid. Luckily, the wings passed over the top of most of the barrels, but I damaged the right wing and knocked a couple of barrels over with the tail section. Fortunately, they didn't explode. My original plan had been to set down right by Jump, but the change in landing direction now put me at the opposite end of the field. I had to taxi back approximately 1,800 feet, in full view of the enemy.

Meanwhile, Paco Vazquez had lost his radio, so he didn't realize what I was up to until after I'd landed. At first he thought I was making a crash landing as well, but when I pulled up after the first attempt and circled for the actual landing, he realized I was going to try for a rescue. He, Hague, and Lucas were providing covering fire by flying almost at ground level between the North Vietnamese and me and Jump. In doing so, they made themselves obvious targets for the enemy.

When I went past Jump, I saw him waving his hands, and I hit the brakes and stopped. He ran behind the airplane, and then I couldn't see him anymore. I waited for him to stick his head up over the canopy, but he didn't appear. That's when I realized I was being peppered with ground fire striking the aircraft, and I figured he must have been hit trying to get to the airplane. I set the brakes and went over the right side to get out and find him. When I climbed out onto the wing, I turned and saw a pair of red eyes staring desperately from the back of the wing. Because the A-1E sometimes stalls when backed off to idling speed, I'd left the engine running fairly fast to make a quick getaway. The airflow over the wing from that big fourteen-foot, four-bladed propeller was literally blowing him off the trailing edge of the wing, and he didn't have the strength to fight against it. I slid back into the left seat and brought the power back to idle, deciding it was worth the risk of a stall.

I moved back to the right seat to help him and looked out in time to see that he'd managed to find the rough coating on the wing where you're supposed to walk and was crawling up on his hands and knees. He made it up to the cockpit and just sort of straddled it, too exhausted to pull himself in. I grabbed him by his flight suit and pulled him into the cockpit headfirst, and he crumpled to the floor. We didn't say much, but he looked up and gave me a weak smile and mumbled something like, "You are one crazy son-of-a-gun." Up until that moment he didn't know that I was the one coming in for the rescue.

Normally we'd strap in, but there was no time for that. The enemy was hitting us pretty hard with small arms fire from just thirty feet away, so I just slid down into the seat and opened the throttle, and away we went, hoping like the dickens that we had enough runway to get airborne. I held the aircraft on the ground until I was almost at the end of the runway. Then I pulled and rotated. The plane came off the ground okay, and we streaked up into the safety of the sky, breaking out of the clouds at about 11,000 feet. When I made it up and off the runway, Paco moved in next to my wing. I brought the aircraft onto a level flight path and then debated whether to go to Da Nang or Pleiku. Pleiku had a better hospital, but the aircraft had been pretty badly hit, and I didn't know if I'd have mechanical trouble. Everything seemed to be operating okay, so I told Jump that if he felt okay, we'd head to Pleiku.

"Whatever you want to do."

So I headed for Pleiku, although I remember thinking: *If it quits on the way, I'll wish like the devil I'd gone to Da Nang.*

I had a couple of canteens of water, which I gave Jump. He asked for a cigarette, but I said, "Sorry, I don't smoke." He looked terrible. He'd tried to camouflage himself by covering his face and hands with mud from the creek, which was foul with oil. It looked like he was burned all over his body from the fiery crash landing, and his clothes were covered in soot from the flames. He smelled awful, but at least he was alive.

We did make it to Pleiku, and I thought to myself, *I am going to land straight on the runway and stop. Forget a pattern.* The moment we touched down, I stopped on the runway as an ambulance raced out to meet us. Two medics jumped up on our wing to help Jump out and into the ambulance, but he refused to get out of the airplane. No matter what they said, Jump just wouldn't move. I don't know why, but he was adamant. So the medics looked him over and said they thought he was okay for a few more minutes and gave me permission to continue to taxi onto the ramp where Jump could get out on his own. I shut it down at the chalk line, and they headed for the hospital.

It turned out that he wasn't burned as badly as I originally believed, which was amazing, considering that his aircraft had started burning while still in the air and his belly tank had exploded on impact. It was a miracle, but he had survived, and we'd made it back to the safety of our airbase.

CHAPTER THIRTEEN

HOW WOULD YOU RATE THIS MISSION?

NEWS OF THE RESCUE SEEMED to gain wings of its own and spread clear across the Southeast Asian command. Although I had a regularly scheduled mission the next morning, it was canceled so that Jump Myers, Paco Vazquez, and I could fly to headquarters to report our version of what happened. When we arrived in Tan Son Nhut, a cadre of reporters was waiting, and the Air Force asked us to speak at an impromptu press conference. It was a huge event, with reporters from Australia, Canada, New Zealand, South Vietnam, Japan, and Great Britain, as well as the United States. Winston Churchill's grandson was one of the reporters, and I was surprised at how much he looked like his famous grandfather.

This was my first experience in meeting with the press, and it was quite disconcerting to be thrust into the role of a hero in such a public way. We described the events at Ashau as best we could, responded to those questions that related to the mission, and assured everyone that we were all okay.

After speaking to the press, we moved to the Southeast Asia "White House" (a three-story Chinese home that served as headquarters) to report to Colonel McGinty of the Office of Air Force Protocol. An amiable man, he asked probing questions about the mission, confirming the levels of risk we had each assumed and the likelihood of a positive outcome. When he finished listening to the story, he turned to me and said, "Bernie, what does this deserve?"

"What do you mean, sir?"

"Well, what do we need to do? You've probably written a citation or two for men under your command. How would you rate this mission compared to some of the others you've read about?"

"Oh, you can't write it on yourself—it's too hard."

"Well, give me some clues as to what you think this is worth."

I was very uncomfortable, but he sat there looking at me expectantly.

"I don't know, but I know somebody that received a Silver Star, and this seems like it might fall into that category."

He smiled and said, "We've just been in touch with the Pentagon, and they concur with our recommendation for the Congressional Medal of Honor. You're the first member of the Air Force to be recommended for service here in Vietnam. What do you think about that?"

It took my breath away. The Medal of Honor is different

than a service medal, which is given at the discretion of each branch of the military. Rather, it is the highest award given to a member of the armed forces, and it is awarded only after a formal nomination is made by the president, who bestows the medal on behalf of the Congress and the people of the United States. I didn't know anyone who had received the Medal of Honor, perhaps because it's usually awarded posthumously. It was originally created to recognize uncommon gallantry and valor during the Civil War. In the succeeding 100 years, it had become the premier symbol of sacrifice and courage above and beyond the call of duty at the risk of one's life in combat. It was a great honor even to be considered for nomination.

I mumbled something of appreciation to the colonel as Jump Myers and Paco congratulated me. I didn't realize at the time the depth of patriotism and gratitude the Medal of Honor inspires in people and had no idea how completely this moment would change my life forever.

I was pleased to learn that the others in our group were nominated for medals as well, and eventually the Silver Star was conferred on Jump Myers and Jon Lucas, and the Distinguished Flying Cross was awarded to Paco Vazquez and Denny Hague.

Being recommended wasn't the same as being accepted, so although it was a great honor, nothing further was said about the nomination, and I was allowed to return to the squadron with Paco and Jump.

As soon as we returned to Pleiku, we hooked up with Jon Lucas and Denny Hague to find out how they were doing. When an incident like Jump's rescue occurs, it's important to capture as much information as possible before memories change or fade, so I invited everyone over to my hooch to talk about it. I had a reel-to-reel tape recorder, and we sat together for more than an hour talking into the microphone to record our individual version of events. It was amazing to hear the others' accounts and to realize how vulnerable Jump and I had been on the ground. Without the other three flying cover, Jump and I definitely wouldn't have made it out alive.

Paco Vasquez described the anxiety he felt while I was sitting on the Ashau runway, waiting as Jump ran to my aircraft. He said it was like watching someone run in slow motion, and he was sure I'd get killed while sitting there waiting. It felt very different to Jump, who says he made the fastest fifty-yard dash in history—at least for a forty-six-year-old.

Jon Lucas (Luke) had taken a direct hit in the pitot navigation system on one of his passes and reported smoke in his cockpit. The damage had knocked out most of his hydraulics. He should have disengaged and headed straight back to the base, but he realized that we were exposed like sitting ducks while I was idling on the airstrip waiting for Jump, so he took a few moments to set up a napalm run with some jet fighters that were already in the valley and made another strafing run to protect us.[1]

Denny was acting as Luke's wingman, and he said they

---

1. See appendix A for a complete transcript of the C-123 audio recording of the rescue at Ashau, including comments by Jon Lucas, Denny Hague, and Paco Vazquez.

had tried to fly low enough that the Vietnamese would be "afraid to stick their heads up for fear the propellers would hit them."

Paco had lost his radio shortly after Jump was forced to ditch, so it took him a while to figure out that I was going to make a rescue attempt. When it did dawn on him what was happening, he was quick to follow Luke and Denny's lead, and the three of them flew strafing runs the whole time I was on the ground. At one point, Luke ordered another pass, and Denny called back that he was "Winchester," which means he was out of ammunition. Luke said that was okay—so was he—but the North Vietnamese didn't know that. So they made a "dry" pass over the enemy without any ammunition. It was particularly courageous given the fact that Luke's aircraft was damaged and difficult to control.

After I had picked up Jump and cleared the airfield, Luke turned his attention to his own problems. Smoke continued to seep into his cockpit, and he worried that he'd have to ditch his aircraft. He hadn't dared let the hydraulics go while flying support for me, because it was simply too difficult to control an A-1E through tight maneuvers on cables alone. After gaining some altitude, he reached down and pulled the hydraulic bypass, which left him with just cables to control the airplane. It's a real challenge to manually pilot such an unwieldy airplane. On the way, Luke told Denny to get out of the way because he was going to jettison his bombs. Denny said that as he watched the erratic movements of the plane, he was certain that Lucas would be forced to ditch on a small dirt airfield a little further up the valley. When Luke released the bombs, however, the aircraft stabilized. Denny flew in close to complete a visual inspection and advised Luke that there was no visible fire coming from the aircraft. Lucas decided to try to make it to a base and headed straight for Da Nang, because it was closer than Pleiku. Denny Hague flew on his wing to help him in. When they arrived at Da Nang, they had to make a non-instrument landing because Luke's instruments were all shot up. Denny guided him in but decided against a joint landing, because he worried that Luke would have trouble in the landing and it would be better to have just one aircraft on the runway if there was a crash. He pulled up and circled out for a delayed landing about three minutes later.

Luke didn't have any problem, though. He made a good, clean landing, then pulled up and shut the engine down on the ramp. As he climbed out of the aircraft, a furious Air Force colonel came racing out in a big blue staff car, jumped out, and started screaming at Luke to get his blankety-blank airplane off the ramp because his hoses were bleeding hydraulic fluid all over the place. Luke had unintentionally pulled onto a VIP white concrete ramp that was purposely kept spotless for arriving dignitaries, and he had made a real mess of it. About that time, Denny Hague completed his 360-degree rollout and landing and started taxiing over to the ramp that Lucas was on. He could see the colonel yelling at Luke and wondered what was wrong. When the colonel spotted Hague, however, he broke off and ran frantically toward Denny's aircraft, screaming at the top of his lungs for Denny to get his bombs out of there. In the confusion of the escape, Denny had failed to jettison two of his bombs, but he didn't know they were still there because they were in a spot where he couldn't see them. When he figured out what the colonel was yelling about, he had to taxi behind some steel revetments so the ground crew could safely unload the bombs.[2]

After things settled down, the maintenance crew at Da Nang towed Lucas's damaged aircraft off the ramp, and he and Denny went to the Officers Club to get something to eat. Partway through, they were interrupted and asked to debrief the mission for intelligence. Apparently, the forward air controller on the scene as well as the crew of the C-123 had reported that something dramatic had happened at Ashau, and Air Force Intelligence wanted a firsthand report.

When they got inside, Denny said something like, "You are not going to believe what we are going to tell you. But, as God is my witness, this is what happened," and then proceeded to tell the story from start to finish.

When they returned to Pleiku an hour or so later, they were amazed to receive an unexpected greeting. Here's what Denny Hague said about it after the debriefing: "Luke jumped into my airplane with me, and by now it was late in the afternoon. We had no bullets left, no bombs, we were just going to fly back to Pleiku, which we did. We taxied in and shut it down, and there was Jump Myers standing on the ramp. His eyes looked like radishes. I mean, he was still in his smoky old flight suit, and his eyes were red from all the smoke and stuff, and he just ran up and gave us both a big hug and a big thank-you."[3]

---

2. From a transcript of a video interview with Jon Lucas and Denny Hague by Nathan and Kelly Fisher. Used with permission.

3. Ibid.

I was amazed to hear about the dry run and everything they'd done to protect me while on the ground. I felt such overwhelming gratitude that these guys had risked their lives to help. They were heroes in the finest sense of the word.[4]

It was a day of miracles for the five of us to make it to safety without even a single serious wound. It was only later, when I was alone, that I realized how much we'd beaten the odds. If just one enemy gunner had changed the angle on the muzzle of his weapon by even a quarter of an inch, any one of us could have been another casualty on the fields of Vietnam. I offered a deeply felt prayer thanking the Lord for protecting us. I think that Denny Hague, a strong Catholic, expressed our feelings well when he said, "I don't know if it's because of a Catholic prayer or a Protestant prayer, but somebody sure helped us today."

Unfortunately, things turned out tragically for the Special Forces defenders on the ground. As I exited the area after picking up Jump, I raised the Special Forces commander on the radio and asked him what we could do to help him. He replied that they needed more men and ammunition because they were staying, but I knew they couldn't really be doing that. They were trying to let one or two men escape from the camp at a time so they could sneak out through the jungle past the North Vietnamese. The Special Forces commander

---

4. The source material for this book comes from several dozen face-to-face and phone interviews between the coauthors in 2002. Because of the complexity of describing this rescue, however, we drew on a number of additional accounts, including two interviews with Bernie Fisher conducted in the years immediately following the rescue. Another source includes information from interviews with Paco Vazquez, General Denny Hague, and Jon Lucas that were granted to Nathan

was just talking brave on the radio in case the enemy was monitoring the broadcast. For the next several days, the Air Force spent a lot of time in Ashau Valley trying to pick up survivors, but the casualty rate was horrific. Out of the hundreds of original camp defenders, it's my understanding that only thirteen of the Special Forces soldiers made it out. There was a lot of tragedy and heroism in their story. One of the men was a medic named Sergeant Hall. He was taking care of the wounded when he got hit with a mortar that took off one of his legs. I understand that he tied a tourniquet of surgical tubing around his wounded leg and then crawled around on the stub trying to take care of people. He apparently lived about fourteen hours after being wounded before he died.

One of the things that made this particular battle unique is that virtually every person in the camp was killed or wounded—basically a 100-percent casualty rate. The battle at Ashau was a military disaster, but not for lack of courage on the part of its American defenders. I only wish we could have done more to help them.

---

and Kelly Fisher for a videotape entitled *Bernie Fisher, Everyday Hero,* for KBYU television.

For a copy of *Bernie Fisher, Everyday Hero,* produced by Kelly Fisher and Nathan Fisher, please consult www.creativeworks.byu.edu or call 1–800–962–8061.

For more information, please refer to:

T. R. Sturm, "Into the Valley of Death," *The Airman* (official magazine of the United States Air Force), March 1967, 4–7. The magazine is published by Information Division, Directorate of Information, Office of the Secretary of the Air Force. Stop B-15, Bolling AFB, Washington, D.C., 20332.

Bernard Fisher, as told to Edward D. Muhlfeld and Robert I. Stanfield, "At the Risk of His Life . . . beyond the Call of Duty," *Popular Aviation,* May/June 1967, 29–34.

Bernie Fisher and Jump Myers after the rescue

South Vietnam with key areas circled, Ashau Valley, Pleiku, Nha Trang, Cam Ranh, and Bien Hoa

The Douglas A1-E Skyraider (photo-illustration by Dennis Millard)

Illustration from the June 4, 1966, Saturday Evening Post *depicting the rescue (© 1966 Curtis Pub. Co., Independence Square, Philadelphia, PA)*

The versatile and durable Douglas A1-E Skyraider that made the rescue possible

The President of the United States of America, authorized by Act of Congress, March 3, 1863, has awarded in the name of the Congress the Medal of Honor to

MAJOR BERNARD FISHER
UNITED STATES AIR FORCE

for conspicuous gallantry and intrepidity in action at the risk of his life above and beyond the call of duty.

Citation: On 10 March 1966, the special forces camp at A Shau was under attack by 2,000 North Vietnamese Army regulars. Hostile troops had positioned themselves between the airstrip and the camp. Other hostile troops had surrounded the camp and were continuously raking it with automatic weapons fire from the surrounding hills. The tops of the 1,500-foot hills were obscured by an 800 foot ceiling, limiting aircraft maneuverability and forcing pilots to operate within range of hostile gun positions, which often were able to fire down on the attacking aircraft. During the battle, Major *Bernard Fisher,* 1st Air Commandos, observed a fellow airman crash land on the battle-torn airstrip. In the belief that the downed pilot was seriously injured and in imminent danger of capture, Major *Fisher* announced his intention to land on the airstrip to effect a rescue. Although aware of the extreme danger and likely failure of such an attempt, he elected to continue. Directing his own air cover, he landed his aircraft and taxied almost the fill length of the runway, which was littered with battle debris and parts of an exploded aircraft. While effecting a successful rescue of the down pilot, heavy ground fire was observed, with 19 bullets striking his aircraft. In the face of withering ground fire, he applied power and gained enough speed to lift-off at the overrun of the airstrip. Major *Fisher's* profound concern for his fellow airman, and at the risk of his life above and beyond the call of duty are in the highest traditions of the United States Air Force and reflect great credit upon himself and the Armed Forces of his country.

THE WHITE HOUSE
January 19, 1967

Official citation awarding Bernie Fisher the Congressional Medal of Honor

One of many publications honoring the events at Ashau Valley

Service medals Bernie Fisher earned through a long and distinguished career

Congressional Medal of Honor

Silver Star

Distinguished Flying Cross

Republic of Vietnam Service

Paco Vasquez, Bernie Fisher, Denny Hague, Jon Lucas

Colonel Bernard Fisher, USAF Retired

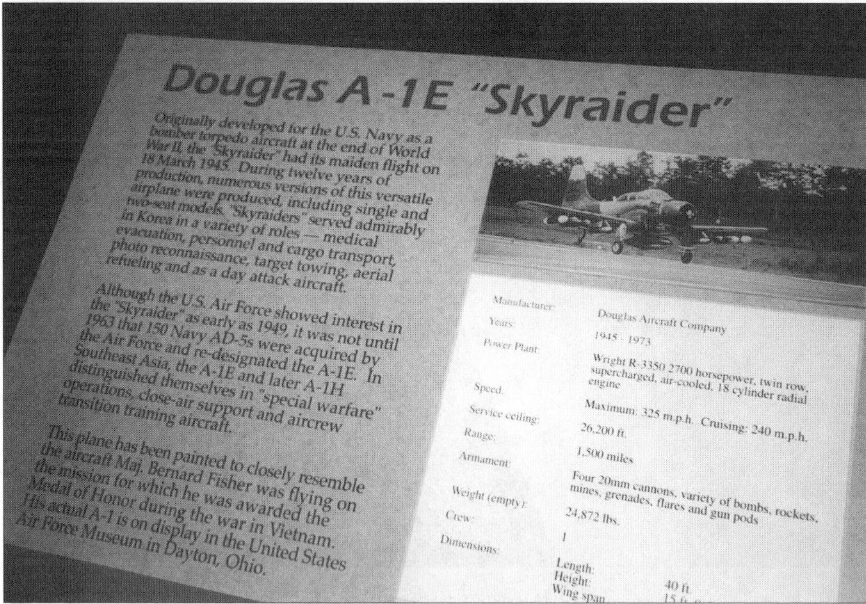

Permanent display at Hill Air Force Base near Clearfield, Utah, where Bernie grew up as a boy

Bernie Fisher standing next to the A1-E Skyraider at Hill Air Force Base near Clearfield, Utah

Bernie and his wife, Realla

Bernie and Jerry Borrowman at Hill Air Force Base

PART 3

INTO THE SPOTLIGHT

CHAPTER FOURTEEN

GERMANY AND THE WHITE HOUSE

In the course of the next few weeks, I flew an additional thirty combat missions in Vietnam that ran the gamut of ground support to rescue missions—nothing I hadn't been doing for the previous nine months. Then I received word that they were building a special composite unit to support a group of B-26 bombers. That would be my next assignment. But before the transfer came through, the group commander called me into his office and asked me to read two regulations that had been brought to his attention. One was a Fifth Air Force regulation, the other an Air Force general regulation. The specific citation he pointed to indicated that Medal of Honor recipients should not be exposed to regular combat assignments. Apparently, if the enemy becomes aware of the individual's special status, they were known to take extraordinary measures to kill that person.

Even though I hadn't been awarded the medal, simply being nominated brought me under the regulations. In order to comply, Group Command was contemplating where to send me while I completed my regular tour. At one point they suggested Vung Tao, which is a resort area like one of the coastal cities in Southern California. Another idea was to send me to Bangkok, Thailand, to work in a manufacturing plant. That sounded pretty bad to me, since I was a pilot, not an engineer.

Finally, the group commander said, "Bernie, why don't we just send you home?" I think he wanted to get me out of his hair.

"Sounds fine with me."

With a crisp salute, he said, "Clear the base and go to the booth for out-processing."

That was the rather abrupt end of my tour of duty in Vietnam. It was okay, though, because I was ready to go home and see my family. I filled out the appropriate papers, they handed me a copy of my flying records, and they cleared me for a flight home through Ton San Nhut. After saying good-bye to my friends, I made the flight and then boarded a troop transport that made approximately four hops to get across the Pacific, with stops in the Philippines, Wake Island, Hawaii, and finally Travis Air Force Base in California. When I arrived at Travis, I exited the aircraft and carried my two bags to Customs to make a connection to a commercial airline to Boise. As I was standing in line, a fellow in a bright orange flying suit came up to me and said, "Are you Major Bernie Fisher?"

"Yes, I am," I replied.

"Then just give your bags to the Customs officer and come with me."

We went outside a door to the east of the Customs office, and he pointed to a T-33 jet trainer with "Air National Guard" written on the side of it.

"Jump in, sir. I've already filed a flight plan, and we're cleared for Boise!"

Pretty nice, I thought, as I climbed into the rear seat. We took off and climbed above the mountains on a direct course for Idaho. About 100 miles out of Boise, a group of four F-102s joined up to escort us into town. I felt honored to receive this recognition. When we arrived in Boise, the formation descended to 1,500 feet, made a pass over Boise, then flew around some of the small towns in southwestern Idaho, including Eagle, Star, and Kuna, where my family lived. After this little air show, we landed at the Boise airfield to be greeted by Realla and the boys, the governor of Idaho, the mayor of Boise, and a crowd of well-wishers who had gathered to welcome me home. I crawled down the ladder and gave Realla a great big hug. Then I turned to say a few words to the crowd. After that, we drove out to our house in the country, and I relished the chance to be alone with my family.

The Air Force granted a thirty-day leave so I could reconnect with my family and honor some of the speaking and appearance requests that started flooding in. We did our best to minimize the importance of the nomination with our boys because we didn't want it to interfere with their normal routines.

I thought the attention would die down quickly, but two

or three requests continued to come in weekly from civic organizations and different groups. People were very anxious about Vietnam and wanted to hear firsthand how things were going there, as well as to learn about the rescue mission. Well-wishers seemed to attribute great significance to the idea that those of us involved would risk our lives to save a grounded pilot, and it struck a patriotic chord to have me speak. It's as if people wanted some tangible way to say thank you for the remarkable blessings we enjoy as Americans, and I became a representative of the great traditions they appreciated. One man took the trouble to drive out to our house in the country, showing up at the doorstep with four chickens that he'd cleaned and prepared. When I answered the door, he looked up rather shyly and said, "There's nothing I can say to thank you except maybe give you some chicken to share with your family."

I thanked him for his kindness and was moved that he felt so strongly about what we'd done. The story seemed to have that kind of effect on people.

Eventually, the demands on my time grew pretty difficult, and I worried that I would become a full-time publicist for the Air Force rather than a pilot. Somehow my problem came to the attention of General McConnell, the chief of staff of the Air Force, and he gave me a call. When I explained to him that it was pretty tough to turn down requests from someone like Idaho's senior senator, Frank Church, he said, "Bernie, from here on out all of your requests will have to come through me. If there's an assignment you want to go to, let me know and we'll clear you. Otherwise, there's no one better than me at sweet-talking people out of a request, and I'll be the one to tell them no, in a nice way." From then on it was up to the chief of staff to decide when and where I spoke.

I received a call asking where I'd like to be stationed. My first choice was as an adviser to the Air National Guard, because that would give me the most time with my family. But at least eighteen months notification is required to get one of those postings, so that was unavailable. Our second choice was to go to West Germany. This request was processed, and I received word to report to Hahn Air Base near Wiesbaden. The boys were excited to go to a new country, so we made the arrangements and headed off for a new adventure.

On the way, I was asked to speak to the Rotary Club of Salt Lake City, Utah. My sisters who lived in the area asked if I'd like to meet President David O. McKay of The Church of Jesus Christ of Latter-day Saints. I was delighted at the possibility, and after giving my talk to the Rotarians, my sisters took me over to church headquarters, where I had the chance to talk with President McKay for a few minutes. He took a keen interest in the story of the rescue and of the opportunities it was creating for me to meet with groups around the country. He had that remarkable white hair that distinguished him, and I felt it was one of the greatest opportunities of my life to stand in the presence of a prophet. In some respects I was an ambassador for the church as well as the Air Force; my membership was always mentioned in articles and introductions.

I was a major at the time we arrived in Germany and was first assigned as the flight commander of a group of eight

F-102 pilots flying for Air Defense Command on the border of East and West Germany. The F-102 Convair Delta Dart is larger and less agile than the F-104 Starfighters I flew in Florida, but it felt great to be back in jet fighters. Flying the A-1E had been a good experience, but I loved the smooth acceleration and graceful maneuverability of a jet fighter.

Germany is a beautiful country, with thick forests and picture-book scenery. Our family easily settled into life on the base, and we started taking German lessons as soon as possible. We enjoyed going into town on the weekends and mixing with the German people. In the summer, we did an exchange program with some area families so a couple of our boys could live in German homes for a period.

Our boys went to American schools with the children of other Air Force personnel, so it didn't require much of an adjustment for them academically. The younger boys were able to live at home and attend school right on the base. When Bradford reached high school age, he had to live in a boarding school in Wiesbaden, since there weren't enough kids in Germany to justify a high school on each individual base. That was a disappointment for us, but Brad seemed to adjust to it okay.

Air Defense in Germany meant flying up and down the corridor that separated East and West Germany. The East Germans let us fly the corridors, but if one of our birds ever drifted into their air space, they'd try to shoot it down. We had to be careful not to accidentally cross over to the enemy side, because Germany is quite small, and the border was just twelve minutes from our base. It was always something of a worry that a pilot might lose his radio or navigation equipment and accidentally get off course.

I made a mistake one day that could have turned into a serious incident. Maintenance had completed some work on my aircraft, and I needed to check it out to make sure all systems were functioning correctly. To do that, I needed to run some intercepts, but there were no other fighters in the air with me at the time, so I just sighted in on the contrails of a commercial jetliner that was flying east. It took some effort to catch him because he was traveling fast—about 525 miles per hour—but I put the power to it and chased him down. I made a couple of passes on the airliner, although he probably didn't even know it. Everything was working fine, and I was having some fun, when it suddenly dawned on me that I'd been in the air for quite a long time and had probably traveled into the wrong sector. A check on my location confirmed that I was definitely in the wrong place. I turned everything off, including radar, and descended closer to the ground to sneak back to Hahn, hoping that no East German fighters would show up. Nothing ever came of it, even though I'm sure they had a track on the ground radar. It was pretty scary until I was back in friendly territory.

Occasionally my flight group flew some missions with the West German Luftwaffe, and I found their pilots and crews to be extremely capable and efficient.

In December 1966, I received a classified message from Washington, D.C., instructing me to report at the White House with my family on January 19, 1967. That was my official notification that the nomination for the Medal of Honor had been confirmed. News of the ceremony created a lot of excitement on the base, and everyone seemed to take pride in the recognition this would bring to the Air Force.

When our travel orders arrived, they indicated that we were to fly back to the United States in an old-style Constellation propeller aircraft. That seemed a little old-fashioned since regular jet service was now available across the Atlantic. But the Protocol Office in Washington assured us that we'd like traveling in this "Special Air Mission" aircraft. It turned out to be the *Columbine,* a four-engine cruiser that had served as President Dwight D. Eisenhower's personal aircraft, and it was a beautifully appointed executive aircraft with swivel seats, wood paneling, and thick carpets on the floor. It even had beds to sleep in. The crew told us to feel free to telephone anyone in the world while we were on board. In other words, we had all the conveniences of the president. What a remarkable way to travel!

We landed at Andrews Air Force Base near Washington, D.C., and were taken to Bolling Field, where we stayed at the Base Officers' Quarters. The Air Force assigned a personal aide to help Realla and me get around the D.C. area to the various receptions and events we needed to attend. They also assigned a captain to each of our boys to take them on tours of the capital while we were out on Air Force business. One of the officers had a Chevrolet convertible, which impressed the boys. When they got to the Washington Monument, the boys said they wanted to climb to the top. One of the captains said, "I'll bet you a dollar I can beat you to the top." So the kids took off up the stairs on a dead run while the captains stayed at the bottom. Apparently it was worth a dollar not to have to climb the stairs.

Plans for the ceremony were reviewed the next day at a special briefing. They'd planned an outdoor parade where I would review each of the five different services—the Army, Navy, Marines, Coast Guard, and the Air Force in party with other officials and dignitaries. The ceremony itself was to take place on the grounds of the White House following the parade.

Unfortunately, it snowed about a foot that night, which is quite unusual for Washington, D.C. The traffic was all snarled up the next morning, so they moved to Plan B, which was to hold the reception at the White House. A limousine picked us up early to make sure we'd arrive on time. In fact, we arrived at 09:50 rather than 10:00, so the driver said, "We'll drive around the block so we can arrive precisely on time."

At exactly 10:00 A.M., we pulled into the portico of the North entrance of the White House, and dozens of well-wishers were there to meet and encourage us as we made our way to the Red Room to wait for the president. The military guards gave a crisp salute as we passed each station. There was a nervous energy in the air while we waited for President Johnson to come into the room, and people whispered, as if it were inappropriate to speak out loud. A hushed silence fell over the room when the president entered, but he didn't seem to notice. Other than a brief acknowledgement of the dignitaries in the room, the president focused his attention on our family, taking a few moments to chat with each of us. When he was ready, he grabbed me by the arm and took off down a short hall, then made a quick right and entered the East Room. That's when it got exciting. It was thrilling to see the effort they'd spent to make it a special occasion. My mother was there, even though she was in ill health because of a heart condition. When notified of her medical problems, the Air Force had dispatched a T-39 executive jet to bring her and my in-laws to the ceremony. They also sent a 131 twin-engine turbo-prop to pick up other family members and friends. I was also gratified to see the other pilots involved in the rescue: Paco Vazquez, Jon Lucas, Denny Hague, and Jump Myers.

The Drum and Bugle Corps played "Hail to the Chief" as we entered the room and walked down a row lined with television cameras and reporters. Just prior to presenting the award, a local artist performed a song written in Vietnam by Captain Richard Robbins that detailed Jump Myers's rescue at Ashau. It was later recorded by Tennessee Ernie Ford, who said, "I think that's a marvelous piece of work—the song story of that gallant rescue mission. Yes, that's how Robbie told the story of the big day at Ashau Valley in South Vietnam. Robbie himself never got home to Mother. Captain Richard Robbins from Cleveland Heights, Ohio, was killed in action not long after he and his guitar had put that song together—killed during an act of heroism which merited the posthumous award of the Silver Star. In his memory, to his widow, Elsa, and their three young sons, Robbie, God bless you."

After the song, President Johnson stepped to the podium to offer his formal remarks:

"We have come here to the East Room this morning to honor Major Bernard F. Fisher of the United States Air Force. He is the first air officer to win the Medal of Honor in

Vietnam. Major Fisher has won this honor, the nation's highest honor, because of uncommon gallantry in the face of death. The action for which we salute him today took place last March and took place during a very bitter and a very bloody battle. Yet, in that battle, it did not involve taking a life, but did involve saving a life. The man that Major Fisher rescued, Lieutenant Colonel Daffort Myers, is here with us today. I should like to point out that this desire to save lives instead of taking lives is not just confined to Major Fisher. It is rather, I think, typical of all of our men in Vietnam. It is particularly true of those who serve with Major Fisher in the most difficult air war in the history of the United States. Like Major Fisher, these men fight with determination, but they hate the killing and they hate the destruction and they hate the waste that are products of war. Like Major Fisher, all of these airmen have accepted an extra risk, and it's not the hazard of flying in the mountainous jungle-covered country, though that is very difficult. It is not the threat of an aggressive, well-equipped, and fanatical enemy, though this is very great. These men are conducting the most careful and the most self-limited air war in history. They are trying to apply the maximum amount of pressure with the minimum amount of danger to our own people. There are no fixed fronts in Vietnam, nothing that really separates friend from enemy, or civilian from military. Through Major Fisher and Lieutenant Colonel Myers and the other flyers in that March mission who are here today, Captain Francisco Vazquez, Captain Jon Lucas, Captain Dennis Hague, I would like, through all of these gallant men, to honor the men of the United States Air Force that are serving us in Vietnam and in that area. Those men in that Air Force are helping us to win a very difficult war. They are helping us to defeat a very treacherous enemy. They are helping a young nation to be free and to be born and to be independent. They are helping their own nation, the United States of America, to honor a pledge and to keep a commitment and make its word good and to be treated and trusted and respected in its alliances. They deserve the best their nation can offer them because they are the best of this nation; thank you very much."

The president then stepped aside as the citation for the Medal of Honor was read by Dr. Brown, secretary of the Air Force. The president then draped the Medal of Honor around my neck. It was a solemn, almost sacred, moment—one I'll never forget. I felt very humbled to stand in the White House, the very heart of our nation, and receive recognition for the work we did as professional airmen in the service of our country.

It was also a very happy moment, because all of us involved were still alive. I was the first Air Force recipient in history who did not receive the award posthumously.

I was also the first person to receive the newly designed Air Force Medal of Honor, which features a five-point star, circled in green laurel leaves and oak leaves, with Lady Liberty in the center of the Star. The medal is suspended from a blue ribbon with thirteen white stars representing the original colonies and supported by a brass bar inscribed with the word "Valor." The first Medal of Honor was struck in 1862. Out of more than two million men and women who served in Vietnam, sixty-six received the Medal of Honor. Only sixteen members of the Air Force (and its predecessor, the Army Air Corps) have received it since air service began.[1] It was the single greatest honor of my life to join the ranks of those brave men and women who went beyond the call of duty at the risk of their own lives to help another person.

After the White House Ceremony, we went to the Pentagon and had a special dinner with the senior officers of the Air Force, as well as all the members of the Idaho Congressional Delegation and other important government and civic leaders. People couldn't have been more gracious in the way they treated us and in the respect they showed to all of us who had flown into Ashau that day ten months earlier.

The next morning we flew to New York City for a ceremony at Gracie Mansion, the official residence of the mayor of New York, where the Honorable John Lindsay presented us with a city Gold Medal. After enjoying a beautiful reception and press conference there, we went to the *Ed Sullivan Show* for a live appearance. He had read about my nomination for the medal ten months earlier and had invited Realla to come to New York at the time. When she and her sister arrived at the airport, she was greeted by Ed Sullivan himself, who had taken the time to drive out to meet her. At the time, he indicated that if the award was approved, he'd like me to appear on the show, and the Air Force cleared this appearance.

It was fascinating to join him. I sat right next to him through most of the show, although they somehow blanked me out when his image appeared on camera until it was time

1. Charles Polanski, Congressional Medal of Honor Society, www.cmohs.org. Last updated October 22, 2002.

to discuss the awarding of the medal. They had a patriotic reading and short film presentation about the rescue mission, and then Ed Sullivan talked with me live before millions of people. At the time, he had one of the highest-rated shows on television.

My story was later told in the June 1966 *Reader's Digest*, as well as in numerous other publications. The interviews for these publications gave me a chance to talk about the many heroic deeds I saw in Vietnam every day as American servicemen reached out to help one another on the battlefield.

All of this attention was exciting but also tiring. After New York City, we'd gone to Philadelphia to appear on several shows there. Realla was pregnant with our sixth child but wasn't due for another month. Perhaps the stress of travel was just too much, because she went into premature labor. We rushed her to a hospital in Washington, D.C., fearful that something was wrong with the baby. The doctors said we didn't need to panic, she just needed to rest a bit, but they wanted to keep her for observation. In time her contractions stopped, and it looked like everything would be okay.

While waiting at the hospital, I got a call from someone by the name of Preston. When the protocol officer asked if I knew anyone by that name, I said, "We had a neighbor in Great Falls, Montana, named Preston." It turns out that it wasn't our neighbor—it was General Preston, the U.S. commander for the entire European Theatre. When I picked up the phone, he said he had dispatched his personal aircraft to take Realla wherever she needed to go—back to Idaho or to Germany—just name the destination. He continued, "We'll have someone take care of the children or let you all stay there in Washington, whatever you want to do." It meant a great deal to know that he was genuinely concerned.

Realla started feeling better, so we took the general up on his offer and returned to Germany via Spain on his personal DC-7 aircraft. Our flight arrived at Hahn Air Base about midnight when the normal ground crew wasn't available. They didn't have a staircase to pull up to the aircraft, just ladders, and that wouldn't work very well for Realla. The crew was resourceful, though, and the pilot stacked a bunch of wooden pallets into a makeshift staircase so she could descend comfortably to the tarmac.

She felt much better being back in our home, and her pregnancy progressed normally. We did our best to help the family settle back into a familiar routine, and I resumed my responsibilities at Hahn Air Base. Invitations to speak at military functions and civic events continued to pour in from both Europe and the United States, so it was impossible to fully regain the life we'd had before. For better or worse, part of my responsibility to the Air Force and the United States was to act as an ambassador of goodwill. It was a new challenge that I had to face, since I was far more comfortable sitting in the pilot's seat than being in front of a microphone.

CHAPTER FIFTEEN

MILITARY LIFE IN EUROPE

THE PEOPLE AT THE HAHN Air Base hospital were excited to have a baby born there, particularly our child, so they did some remodeling of the delivery room so it would be more comfortable. As the day approached, I was asked to speak at a Boy Scout function about seventy miles away. Realla accompanied me, and on the way home she went into labor. I raced down the Autobahn to get back to Wiesbaden. When we made it to the city limits, I looked for the first car I could find that displayed the official "U.S." seal on it. As soon as I spied one I flagged it down.

"We need to get to a hospital fast," I said. "My wife is going to have a baby."

"Just go down to the end of this block, turn right and go through the alley—"

"We've got to get there right now!"

The driver saw the seriousness of the situation and said, "Follow me."

We arrived at the hospital in the nick of time, and the medical staff said, "You've got to go to your airbase for this," but when they checked out Realla, they realized there wasn't time to go to the base. Steven was born in a German hospital, giving him dual citizenship. The people at Hahn were kind of disappointed that Realla didn't get to use the room prepared for her.

Shortly after getting back to Germany, our base participated in a biannual European NATO competition called the AFCENT Competition. Each nationality paired up with a squadron from another country to compete in three exercises, such as flying intercepts on a target at 35,000 feet, assessing piloting skills in scrambling and reacting to changing battle conditions, firing accuracy, and so on. It was interesting because each nation flew their preferred aircraft in the shoot-off, so we got to see lots of different birds in action. The French flew the Mirage, the Germans the F-104, the Americans the F-102, the Swedes SAAB's, and so forth. On this occasion, our guys paired up with a German Luftwaffe Squadron, and they did very well. It's a real honor to win even one of the three competitions, but that year we won all three! My flight wasn't assigned to participate, but it was exciting to see our team win. The trophy was about as big as a twin bed.

The position of operations officer opened up at the 525th Squadron, a sister squadron to the 496th. The operations officer is responsible for four flight commanders, flight scheduling, and maintenance. I was ready for a change, so I traveled to Bitburg, Germany, and applied for the post. My application was accepted, and I was promoted to lieutenant colonel with responsibility for the four flight groups. Six months later, the squadron commander finished his tour of duty, and I was appointed to assume his position. The operations officer and maintenance officer were my direct reports, with more than 720 men under my command. It was a challenge, but I thoroughly enjoyed it. In spite of the administrative duties, I was still able to spend a lot of time flying by delegating appropriately so the people who reported to me worked at full efficiency.

Flying in Europe was interesting because of the national rivalries. For weapons certification, we had to fly to North Africa once a year to fire live rockets on a practice range. To get there, we had to pass through a number of countries' airspace on the way. On one occasion we spent about two hours flying over France on our way to the Mediterranean. When we crossed into Italian airspace, we had difficulty understanding the Italian air controllers. Their English was broken and halting, barely adequate to help us land in Aviano, Italy, for refueling and maintenance. Shortly after takeoff for North Africa, one of the pilots in our group developed a problem in the liquid oxygen converter that provides breathable air, and he had to drop to less than 10,000 feet to have enough natural oxygen. I declared an emergency so my pilot could find the closest runway. The Italian air controller came back on the air and spoke to us in beautifully precise and understandable English, giving him the vectors to the nearest base. It shocked me to hear this same controller who was almost unintelligible just a few minutes earlier suddenly speak so clearly. My feeling was that he had been purposefully difficult during normal flight conditions, most likely because he didn't like Americans, but he showed his true abilities when there was an emergency.

In addition to speaking at military functions, I also received invitations to speak to LDS church groups. After speaking at a European Area Conference, the Young Men's leadership of the LDS Church in Europe invited me to speak in Turkey. I needed to provide some in-flight training to a number of pilots anyway, so I went to the wing commander to request permission to take three aircraft cross-country to Athens.

"I have no problem with you going, but you'll never receive diplomatic authority to cross their airspace. You'd need ambassadorial clearance."

"Is it all right if I try to get clearance?"

"Go ahead and try, but it's never been approved."

I called the church contact in Turkey, and he said, "Just a minute, the ambassador is right here." The ambassador gave clearance on the spot, and the trip was approved.

This actually provided the opportunity I'd been looking for to train three of our weaker pilots and give them experience flying near hostile territory. One of the young pilots had previously served as a navigator on a B-58 bomber, where he did fine, but he was having trouble adjusting to Air Defense. He'd get sick when flying close to Soviet territory, a condition the flight surgeon blamed on a simple case of nerves because of the Soviets' propensity to scramble on even the slightest mistake on our part. The doctor told me it would be good to give him some flying time outside the corridor. We filed a flight plan and took off for Turkey through Italy, around the Cape and into Athens, Greece, flying at night to improve the value of the exercise. There's a stretch of about 150 miles where there are no navigational aids—the pilot has to rely exclusively on his radar scope to see where the islands are—making the trip a particularly challenging workout for the pilots. When we got to Athens, I pitched out and made the first landing. One of the young pilots came in too fast and had to "stand on the brakes" to get stopped, which blew out both tires. There were no facilities to replace them in Greece, so he had to wait with the aircraft while replacements were flown in from Germany. The rest of us went on to the fireside at Incerlik Air Base in Turkey. We connected back up with him on the return trip.

One of the most interesting speaking invitations I received was from President N. Eldon Tanner of the First Presidency of the LDS Church. He called me in Germany and asked if I could speak at a Boy Scout function at the Tabernacle on Temple Square in Salt Lake City. I was pleased to oblige and made arrangements to fly back to the United States on space-available travel. It was a wonderful event, and the tabernacle was packed with young Scouts and their adult leaders. The church also arranged for Jump Myers, Denny Hague, and Jon Lucas, to be there, and we talked about America and the patriotic pride we felt in serving our country. The leaders of the church showed us the greatest respect, and I had to chuckle at Denny Hague, my active Catholic friend, because he said, "Bernie, this is just too much. I can't wait to get back and tell my priest all about this!"

My family enjoyed our time in Germany. The boys played sports on the base, and Brad and Courtney became avid soccer players. One summer, we took an extended camping vacation through Germany, Switzerland, and Italy. The boys got to the point that they could set up our tent trailer with everything ready to start dinner in less than ten minutes. Europe has some of the most stunning scenery in the world, particularly through the Swiss and Italian Alps. The mountains are extremely rugged, and at one point the only way to gain passage was to load our car on a railroad train and go through a tunnel to the other side. It was certainly a trip to remember.

Another interesting experience was crossing into East Germany. As an American officer in uniform, I could pass through Checkpoint Charlie in Berlin without having to give any identification to the East Germans whatsoever. That was part of the treaty that divided Germany into four occupied zones at the end of World War II, with Russia responsible for the East German side. Uniformed men of any of the Allied Countries (England, United States, France, and Russia) could pass unchallenged between the various zones. But if I approached as a civilian, the East Germans had the authority to insist on identification and visas. To provide a unique cultural experience, I obtained permission to take a group of Explorer Scouts from the base into East Berlin on a field trip, and it was interesting to see the difference on the eastern side of the Berlin Wall. Life behind the Iron Curtain wasn't nearly as prosperous as it was in West Germany, and the young men were struck by the benefits of capitalism. Going into East Berlin was like going back in time to the 1950s based on the way the people dressed, the cars they drove, and the way the stores were organized. I think we all gained a greater appreciation for the lifestyle we enjoyed as citizens of a free and open society.

A remarkable career opportunity presented itself when I received an invitation to try out for the world famous Thunderbirds, the Air Force's premier precision flying team. All pilots in the Air Force learn to fly in close formation because it conserves air space and increases the team's ability to defend itself. Flying in close formation takes a great deal of concentration, because there are times when your wings are literally within a few feet of each other—often at speeds in excess of 500 miles per hour! It was a thrilling challenge for me, particularly when executing tight turns or high-speed maneuvers. The chance to fly with the Thunderbirds was a once in a lifetime opportunity, and I jumped at the chance.

After passing the Thunderbirds' initial test in Germany, they invited me go to Dallas, Texas, for a more rigorous competition. It was incredible to spend two weeks flying in the backseat with members of the Thunderbird team. They were amazingly precise and totally disciplined in their flying. At the end of each mission, they'd go through an extensive critique of every move they had made during the exercise and make changes to the routine so it was perfect. They seemed to be so experienced that one would think this wouldn't be necessary, but they were religious about it. On a few occasions, they allowed those of us in the backseat to take the controls and fly. That was a real thrill.

After two weeks of orientation and joint flying, they narrowed the candidate list down to just me and one other pilot and instructed us to report at Nellis Air Force Base in Las

Vegas, Nevada. I don't know if it was my flying or behind-the-scenes political maneuvering on the part of the other pilot, but he got the nod. I felt bad about not making the team, but when I returned to Germany, my wing commander told me that even though he'd recommended me for the tryout, he was glad I didn't make it. He knew that membership on the team wouldn't fit my family's lifestyle. The Thunderbirds were always out on the road flying unusual hours, particularly on holidays. His words helped me feel better. It was certainly exciting to get that close and experience firsthand the remarkable skill of those pilots.

At the end of three years, the Air Force announced that they intended to phase out the F-102 Delta Darts in the European Theatre and replace them with F-4 Phantoms. That presented me with a choice: spend at least another year in Europe making the transition, or request a transfer back to the United States. I thought it would be interesting to work through the transition, but the boys were anxious to return to America. They had enjoyed being in Germany, but it was hard to be away from home that long. After holding a family council, I ended up requesting a transfer back to the United States. The first opening that presented itself was in Duluth, Minnesota, flying in an F-106 squadron. The F-106 is a lot like the F-102, but it's a bigger and newer airplane, and I looked forward to certifying on it. We said our good-byes and prepared for a new chapter in our lives in the northern plains of America.

CHAPTER SIXTEEN

TRANSITION FROM MILITARY TO CIVILIAN LIFE

After settling my family, I reported to Duluth Air Force Base and then flew to Tyndall Air Force Base in Florida to certify on the F-106. It was a terrific aircraft, with more electronics than any I'd previously flown. I was out with my instructor one day when a couple of Navy F-4 Phantoms flew past. I was curious about the difference between the Phantom and the F-106, so I said to my instructor, "Why don't we go get those guys?"

Normally that was prohibited, because an unexpected chase could develop into a dangerous situation, but he decided it would be okay, so he said, "Sure, go ahead."

I hit the burner and streaked after them. They saw me coming, and they split, one going down, the other going up. I went after the high man and stayed on his tail through a series of complicated maneuvers as he tried to lose me. No matter what he tried, though, he couldn't get away, which was pretty gratifying to me. We were flying hot, but I learned that the F-106 could outmaneuver and outturn the Phantom. Both aircraft had a great time, and we broke off the encounter with a signal of goodwill to each other. Then I returned to the regular routine of my training mission.

At the end of the mission I got a little worried when I saw a staff car on the tarmac waiting for us to land. The crew chief jumped up on the side of the aircraft and said, "Boy, that was a great show!"

I hadn't realized that we'd given chase close enough to the base for everyone on the ground to watch. It was a pretty foolish thing to do. Then the crew chief said, "Somebody wants to see you down at the command post right away."

I gulped and thought, *There go my wings!* But they wanted me for an entirely different reason, and no one ever said anything about our little contest with the Navy.

Back in Duluth, I had to learn a new skill. Because our territory was significantly larger than on any of my previous assignments, we learned to refuel the aircraft in-flight from a KC-135 orbiting in the area. It was an interesting process that required steady nerves and concentration. You first slide into position approximately twenty-five feet below the tanker, and then a boom operator lying on his belly maneuvers the refueling boom into position by manipulating two wings on the nozzle. He essentially flies the boom with these wings. Once he's ready, he activates a mechanism that attaches the boom to the fighter with a set of claws and then starts pumping fuel. There are five electric lights on the belly of the tanker that he uses to signal to the fighter pilot while they are connected—green, red, white, and two amber lights. It's inevitable during the course of refueling that the two aircraft are always moving slightly in relation to one another, but as long as the fighter is within tolerance, the light stays green. As the fighter takes on more fuel, the aircraft gets heavy and slows down relative to the tanker, so the pilot needs to continually adjust the throttle to add more power. If the fighter fails to stay in position, the operator switches to the amber lights, which warns the pilot to take immediate corrective action or he'll activate the red light and disconnect before he spins the boom and damages it. A bit nerve-wracking, but I was glad to master this new skill because it allowed us to stay airborne for much longer periods.

One of our assignments at Duluth Air Force Base was to provide additional personnel for the five Air Defense bases in Alaska. The threat of Russia launching an attack across the Bering Straits was considered probable enough that Alaska was classified as a first line of defense. The base was too remote for pilots to stay on permanent assignment, so it was staffed on rotation. The members of my team took turns flying our F-106s to McCord Air Force Base in Seattle, Washington, followed by a commercial flight to Anchorage and a helicopter ride out to the remote air base. We'd be in Alaska ten days and then back to Minnesota for twenty days. I enjoyed flying over the remote wilderness of Alaska while on assignment there, but like most pilots didn't like being away from my family for such extended periods.

My real goal at Duluth was to get transferred to a posting as an adviser to the Air National Guard, preferably at the 124th Fighter Group in Boise, Idaho. An adviser remains on active duty as an Air Force officer with full rank and pay but in a supporting role for the reserve pilots in the National Guard. When the job opened up in Boise, my division commander wrote a letter of recommendation that helped me secure the transfer, along with a promotion to the rank of full colonel. Our family was thrilled to go back to Idaho.

As an adviser to the Air National Guard, my responsibilities were quite different than when I supervised full-time Air Force personnel. The men who flew in this command were "weekend warriors" who worked downtown during the week, then flew on weekends and during summer camp. They were all retired Air Force pilots who stayed in service to help out in the event of an emergency. Even though it was a part-time job, they were subject to being activated at any time, which could interfere with employment or vacation plans. That was a price they were willing to pay to give the military the reserve strength it needs to protect the country. Mostly, I think, they just loved the opportunity to continue flying. I had a lot of opportunities to go up in the air with them to ensure that their skills stayed sharp, which I enjoyed immensely too.

After three years in Boise, it was time to rotate, and I was offered a transfer to the Special Missions Alternate Command Post at Ulner Air Force Base in Alaska. It was a good posting from a career point of view, with the next transfer after that likely to earn me a promotion to the rank of general, but my family wouldn't be able to come with me to Alaska. Three years apart was simply too discouraging to even consider. I also knew it would lead to more administrative assignments instead of flying. So, after twenty-seven years, we decided it was time to retire. It was quite a step, and Realla and I questioned it more than once, but the truth is I'd done about everything I wanted to in the Air Force, and it was a good time to leave.

I doubt that anyone has ever enjoyed a career more than I enjoyed my time in the Air Force. I'd flown some of the fastest airplanes in the world to distant locations all over the globe. My job gave my family rare opportunities to experience other people and cultures. So I was content with the decision to step aside and move on to new opportunities. My commander accepted my request and scheduled a retirement party at Mountain Home Air Force Base to the east of Boise. Many of our friends came to pay their regards, and it was a terrific evening sharing lots of memories.

With my Air Force pension as a backup, we decided to take up farming and arranged to buy my father-in-law's farm. We also built a comfortable brick home on the property and settled into life as Idaho farmers. The Boise area has a moderate climate, and we raised corn seeds, sugar beets, beans, wheat, and alfalfa. We've been on the farm since 1971. I rent most of it out to another farmer now that I'm in my mid-seventies, but there are still a lot of things that have to be done, such as maintaining the fences and corrals and keeping the water systems in good repair. Taking care of the farm gives me tasks to occupy my time.

About two years after my retirement, a member of my elder's quorum said he was going to start a small regional airline and wanted to know if I'd be interested in flying with him.

"You bet!" I replied without hesitation.

That was the time when airline deregulation was coming into effect to give small airlines a chance to fly in niche markets that were unprofitable to the larger carriers. Idaho is such a small market that it seemed like a good opportunity. When the new airline was formally chartered and ready to begin business, the owners purchased two Brazilian-built Embrair Air eighteen-passenger turbo-prop airplanes for $1,500,000 each (much lower than the cost of similar American-built aircraft). Another pilot and I flew by commercial airline to Brazil to pick the first plane up. The return trip would require nine stops for fuel along the way, including a scheduled stop in the middle of the Amazon jungle. As we set out, the manufacturer gave us the coordinates for what they described as a well-stocked airfield at Port Nacional that would have everything we needed. They also provided a special radio frequency we should use to alert the ground crew of our impending arrival.

Everything seemed in order, and we left without delay. As we reached the appointed location, however, we couldn't raise anyone on the radio. When I arrived at the place where the airport was supposed to be, all I could see was a red dirt strip. *That can't possibly be the landing field,* I thought to myself. There were no buildings, no facilities, nothing. But we did see a fuel truck off to one side, and our navigation was solid, so we lined up and throttled the airplane down to a dusty landing. We got out of the aircraft to stretch our legs and told the man in charge we'd like to fuel up.

"No problem, señor."

I explained that we wanted to pay by American Express, and he said, "No way—we only take the Bank of Brazil."

"But, we don't have a Bank of Brazil check or card—our American Express card is good, though."

"Bank of Brazil or nothing—that's all I take."

Talk about being marooned in the middle of nowhere! We were about as far away from an alternate airfield as we could possibly be. My partner asked if there was a phone he could use to call the manufacturer to see if they could help us out, but he was told the nearest phone was down in the village. He started to walk down there while I waited with the airplane.

Meanwhile, the Brazilian fellow kept looking at my watch. It wasn't anything special—a Timex, I think. I noticed him looking at it and said, "Do you like this watch?"

"Yes, that's a very fine watch."

"It's yours—I'll give it to you."

"How much?"

"It won't cost you anything. I'll just give it to you."

At that he turned to a two-stripe corporal and said, "Gas 'em up."

When they finished filling our airplanes, I asked how much we owed, and he said, "That's okay, the watch is good enough."

I couldn't believe it. Of course, I insisted that he take our American Express for the cost of the gas, because it would be unfair to the owners of the base not to pay for it. We had no further problems and made it home to Boise without incident.

I flew with Mountain West Airlines for the next four years. Boise was our home base connecting to six destinations in southern Idaho and northern Utah, including

Pocatello, Hailey, Sun Valley, Idaho Falls, Twin Falls, and Salt Lake City. After a couple of years we got additional landing rights in Reno, Nevada.

I enjoyed the work because it was casual and relaxed. I'd show up, take my jacket off and hang it on a hook behind the pilot's seat, roll up my sleeves, and fly the airplane. They were great little airplanes that were easy to control.

Eventually the price of fuel rose to the point that our owner started having financial problems, and the company was taken over in a merger that didn't work out very well. But it was a great experience while it lasted.

I wasn't ready to give up flying, so I accepted a position with a freight company, Regional Express. I would take off from Boise at 23:00 to fly east to Hailey to pick up fuel and freight and then drop south to Twin Falls and on to Salt Lake City. We'd transfer the freight to FedEx, and I'd get home about daylight the next morning. It was pretty exhausting.

I got to thinking one day, *This is ridiculous. Most of the guys who fly these graveyard shifts are trying to build up hours so they can move onto something better. But I don't need any additional hours, so why do I put up this?* The only reason, of course, was that I loved flying. At one point I was flying up to seven missions per day, and I learned to fly with more precision than I ever did in the Air Force because I was in the air so much. Eventually the schedule just wasn't worth the trouble, though, so I asked to be released after about a year.

That was the last professional flying I did, but I've continued to fly small airplanes through the years, finding any number of excuses to go up in the air. For example, my son Brad is my next-door neighbor, and on Fridays he liked to take a morning off from work and go fishing with me in the Idaho wilderness area. We would take off before daylight, arrive just at sunrise at a little spot accessible only by air, get in a few hours of fishing, and fly back to Boise by noon.

One of the most unusual events of our life was to participate in the commissioning of an Air Force forward supply ship that was named in my honor. Realla christened the U.S.S. *Bernard Fisher* by breaking the traditional bottle of champagne across the bow. Through the years, the crew has stayed in touch to let me know of some of the service they offer to aircraft in remote locations.

In 1990, Realla and I were thinking about going on a mission for our church, but too many obligations kept coming up. I was doing farm work down the lane from our house one day when I looked up to see black smoke coming out from under the eaves in the roof of our house. I ran to the house as quickly as I could and saw that the smoke was pouring out of the garage. I rushed inside and saw sparks in the electrical panel, but I couldn't get to it in time to prevent a major fire. A neighbor called the fire department, and even though they got there in about five minutes, the fire spread so quickly that they couldn't save the house. We had a cedar shake roof that I'd put oil on through the years to keep down mold and mildew, and it just went up like an inferno.

We got everyone out of the house safely, but all the mementos I'd collected through the years were in a room in our basement. I tried to get the fire chief to let me in, but the danger was too high—better to let it burn than to endanger someone's life. Fortunately, I was able to get the Medal of Honor out before we lost the house.

With the remains of the house nothing more than a smoldering pile of embers, there was nothing to keep us from going on a mission. We cleaned up most of the rubble and put our papers in for a full-time mission. We were called to serve in the Denver Temple for a twelve-month mission and had a great experience there.

As we walked up the slight incline to the Denver Temple one morning, Realla asked why my hands were trembling. I hadn't noticed anything, but she was more observant with her nursing background. When the trembling didn't subside, I arranged to be checked. The doctor said I was in the early stages of Parkinson's disease. Fortunately, they have some great medicine that has helped suppress the trembling, and I've been able to live a good, full life in spite of it. Since it's a progressive disease, the effects have gotten worse with the passage of time. If I know I have an appointment coming up, I can take the medication and quiet my hands down, but I tend to get fatigued quite easily. Sometimes it's hard to understand me when I first start speaking. I'm still able to drive, although I stay in the right-hand lane since my reflexes aren't what they once were.

In the nearly four decades that have passed since I earned the Medal of Honor, I've spoken at more than 500 events around the world. I always talk about how it takes teamwork and a willingness to put other people's interests ahead of our own to accomplish great things. People sometimes ask why I went down for Jump Myers when my own death was almost a foregone conclusion. That's a difficult question to answer. I understood the risk but felt I couldn't stand by and watch a man get killed. An incident from my youth has haunted me through the years and perhaps had bearing on my actions in Vietnam. A group of friends asked me to go swimming with them at a lake near Clearfield, Utah. It was early spring, and the water was very cold. As we reached the center of the lake, Jack Green, the youngest in the group, called out that he was having trouble. I turned with the others and started swimming toward him as his head went under the water. We frantically dove under the surface to help him, but the water was too murky to see him. One of the guys actually touched him for a moment but couldn't get a solid grip, and Jack slipped from his hand. I surfaced and swam to the nearest shore as fast as I could, ran to the nearest car with keys in it, and raced back to our high school for help. A search party was organized, but it was too late to save Jack. I've never forgotten the despair we felt watching our friend perish without being able to help him. I've thought of the panic that must have gone through his mind as he realized he was in trouble. At Ashau Valley, I simply had to try. With the Lord's help and support from Paco, Jon, and Denny, the rescue was successful. But even if it had turned out differently, it was the right thing to do.

I also encourage people to pray for our leaders so they can avoid war if possible. War is death and destruction, and it takes a terrible toll on those who fight it. But in a world where evil men are opposed to the freedoms we value in America, we need brave men and women in the armed services to protect the rights we cherish. I'm proud that my family continues to be connected to the service as four of our six sons spent time in the military, three choosing careers in the Air Force. I'm also proud to have a grandson who is now in pilot training. It's a tradition worth continuing.

During the first Gulf War, General Dixon invited me to fly to Germany and England to speak to all the fighter groups. I had the opportunity to speak at twelve bases, mostly to fighter pilots like me. As I felt the nervous energy of the men and women getting ready to go into combat, it reminded me of my days in Vietnam when I felt those same emotions. At Ramstein Air Base, one of the general officers took me to the flight line to introduce me to the C-5A pilots that were taking matériel to the war zone. Their work had already started, and they were flying twelve hours straight to get supplies to the troops on the frontlines. It was a particular honor to sit and talk with these pilots and give them some encouragement.

In 2002, something much worse than Parkinson's struck our household. Realla was doing some paperwork in the bedroom while I was working outside. When I came in later, I found her lying unconscious on the floor. She had suffered a stroke and was in a coma for nearly a month. I've never felt so forlorn, and I prayed fervently for her. One day, she finally began to come around. It soon became obvious that she'd been paralyzed by the stroke. She was frustrated being so totally helpless, but she's a strong person, and her recovery has gone far better than the doctors ever imagined. She talks well now, although a little slower than normal. She remains completely paralyzed and needs daily assistance from some wonderful caregivers and members of our family. I suppose we could just surrender to these problems, but it doesn't make sense to withdraw from life. Instead, we get out into the community as often as we can. I bought a van that accommodates a wheelchair, and with help from family and caregivers we go to church each Sunday and to a seniors family home evening once a month. It's difficult, but we do the best we can.

Several years ago a friend of mine, Larry Reader, talked to me about ultralight airplanes. These are small aircraft weighing no more than 350 pounds and sporting an open-air seat to give the pilot an unparalleled view of the country-side. With a takeoff speed of only twenty-five miles per hour and a top speed of fifty-five, it's flying in its purest, simplest form. It's about as close to being a bird as a person can ever get. I was fascinated as I always have been, so we decided to go in together and buy a Nomad, one of the best available. I built a metal barn to house the airplane, and we could go right out the back door of my house and take off in the field. I loved flying up and down the country lanes and out over my neighbors' fields.

About a year ago, Larry came over to take the plane up for awhile. We brought it out of the barn and fueled it up, and Larry took it up in the air. After he landed, I decided to take a turn, so I strapped myself onto the metal bar the pilot sits on and started it up. I was going down the hayfield approaching lift-off speed when I decided things just didn't feel right. With my Parkinson's disease, I didn't have the level of control that I wanted, so I stopped the airplane, got out, walked back to the barn, and said, "Larry, I don't think I'll fly it anymore."

Larry smiled a sad sort of smile, but he didn't try to talk me out of it. He offered to buy my half interest and moved the airplane down to a little airport in the area. It was a poignant moment for me. It had been nearly sixty-two years since my first flight with Haven Barlow. Now my time as a pilot had come to an end. How grateful I am for those wonderful years I was in the air. I've truly been blessed with an abundant life.

APPENDIX A

SUPPORTING ACCOUNTS AND CITATIONS

OFFICIAL CITATION OF THE AWARDING OF THE MEDAL OF HONOR

THE PRESIDENT OF THE UNITED States of America, authorized by Act of Congress, March 3, 1863, has awarded in the name of the Congress the Medal of Honor to

Major Bernard Fisher
United States Air Force

for conspicuous gallantry and intrepidity in action at the risk of his life above and beyond the call of duty.

Citation: On 10 March 1966, the Special Forces camp at Ashau was under attack by 2,000 North Vietnamese Army regulars. Hostile troops had positioned themselves between the airstrip and the camp. Other hostile troops had surrounded the camp and were continuously raking it with automatic weapons fire from the surrounding hills. The tops of the 1,500-foot hills were obscured by an 800-foot ceiling, limiting aircraft maneuverability and forcing pilots to operate within range of hostile gun positions, which often were able to fire down on the attacking aircraft. During the battle, Major Bernard Fisher, 1st Air Commandos, observed a fellow airman crash-land on the battle-torn airstrip. In the belief that the downed pilot was seriously injured and in imminent danger of capture, Major Fisher announced his intention to land on the airstrip to effect a rescue. Although aware of the extreme danger and likely failure of such an attempt, he elected to continue. Directing his own air cover, he landed his aircraft and taxied almost the full length of the runway, which was littered with battle debris and parts of an exploded aircraft. While effecting a successful rescue of the downed pilot, heavy ground fire was observed, with 19 bullets striking his aircraft. In the face of withering ground fire, he applied power and gained enough speed to lift-off at the overrun of the airstrip. Major Fisher's profound concern for his fellow airman and at the risk of his life above and beyond the call of duty are in the highest traditions of the United States Air Force and reflect great credit upon himself—and the Armed Forces of his country.

Lyndon B. Johnson
THE WHITE HOUSE
January 19, 1967

SERVICE MEDALS AND AWARDS EARNED IN BERNIE FISHER'S MILITARY CAREER

The Congressional Medal of Honor
The Silver Star
The Distinguished Flying Cross
The Air Medal (awarded on eight separate occasions)
The Combat Readiness Medal
The American Defense Service Medal
The World War II Victory Medal
The National Defense Service Medal
The Armed Forces Expeditionary Medal
The Vietnam Service Medal
The Air Force Longevity Service Award Ribbon
The Small Arms Expert Marksmanship Ribbon

TRANSCRIPT OF C-123 AUDIO RECORDING

THE C-123 STARTED THEIR audio recording after Bernie Fisher had made the decision to attempt a rescue.

Unknown Voice: He's about twenty feet.

Another Unknown Voice: Understand he's twenty feet.

Fisher: Roger.

Lucas: Which way you gonna land?

Fisher: I'm gonna make a 180-degree, come in to the southeast.

Lucas: Okay. Well then, we'll come in behind and strafe parallel to your heading.

Fisher: Okay, I'm rolling in now.

Unknown Voice: Make it slow or you'll lose it.

Lucas: I'm right behind you, Bernie. I took a hit in my pitot system, and I'm smoking a little.

Hague: Okay, Luke, I'm right back at your six o'clock.

Lucas: Do you see any smoke?

Hague: Negative. You look pretty good.

Lucas: Okay, my air speed's gone, and my hydraulic pressure's fluctuating.

Hague: All right. You want me to stay with you?

Lucas: Okay, Bernie, you gonna land on this pass?

Fighter on top at 20,000 feet: 5-2 [call sign], this is 81, over.

FAC: [Call sign] 5-2.

Fighter: We're overhead your position for pylon turn at 1,240. We're ten minutes late. We have 500 CPs and 20 mike-mike [eight 500-pound general-purpose bombs and 20-milimeter cannon].

FAC: All right, sir, hold high and dry. At the present time, we have A-IE's working underneath. There's an aircraft down in there, and we're trying to get the pilot out.

Fighter: This is 07-1 [call sign]. We're still orbiting up here at 20,000.

FAC: Roger, hold high and dry now, sir.

Fighter: Roger.

Fighter: Now 5-2, this is Crandall 56 with eight napes [napalm] and eight bombs and 20 mike-mike.

FAC: Roger, stand by. The weather underneath is not too good for napalm at the present time.

Fighter: Roger.

Lucas: Okay, Paco, are you in trail with us now?

[No response; Vazquez was evidently having radio trouble.]

Unknown Voice: Zero three, uh, shoe-shine zero three.

Lucas: Roger, go ahead, Jim [fighter pilot].

Jim: Roger, which kind of help do you need? We're three miles up the valley.

Lucas: Okay, Jim, do you read me?

Jim: I hear ya.

Lucas: Okay, babe, come on down the valley. As you come down the valley, you run over that airstrip, pick up a heading of one five zero. You can run the napalm right down the east side of the runway.

Jim: Understand. One-fifty down the east side of the runway. Okay, got that, Pete?

Pete [Jim's wingman]: Roger dodger, Jim.

Lucas: You'll see quite a bit of smoke.

Jim: Okay, I see an aircraft down there to the left. Who's that? You?

Lucas: No, I'm coming down the east side of the runway now. Why don't you come down one time and look it over.

Fighter: Okay, this is Hobo 21. We're up here, Luke.

FAC: Hobo 21, Bird dog 52.

Fighter: Roger, 52. We're orbiting the airfield to the north at 6,000 feet.

Lucas: Okay, let's hit everything, Denny, except the fort.

Hague: Roger, I gotcha . . . but I'm Winchester [out of ammunition].

Lucas: Okay, so am I. Let's keep making passes, though. Maybe they don't know it.

Hague: Roger.

Lucas: Okay, Jim. The area's smokin' pretty badly, and you'll see an aircraft burning on the runway. Bernie's taking off to the north.

Jim: Okay, understand to the north. Okay, I can see him. Is he rolling now?

Hague: Roger-roger.

Lucas: Okay, get the east side, Denny.

Hague: Roger-roger, Babe.

Jim: Where do you want those trenches strafed, Jon?

Lucas: Okay, you got us in sight? We're breaking off. I'm coming left.

Jim: Where do you want the strafe to? Right on the east end of the runway?

Lucas: Yeah, put it all down the east side of the runway, in the grass area. Put a couple of bursts in there and then get hold of Barry.

Jim: Get hold of who?

Lucas: Correction, it'll be Hound Dog 12 if he's still up.

Jim: Okay, right here, we'll be coming right in now.

Lucas: All the gunfire is over here on the east side in these trees.

Jim: Luke, you got a chopper comin' in up here to the north. Uh, he may be able to get the pilot out.

Lucas: We already got him out. [!]

Jim: Roger.

EYEWITNESS ACCOUNTS OF THE RESCUE

THE FOLLOWING ACCOUNTS ARE summarized from interviews with Jon Lucas, Paco Vazquez, and General Denny Hague that were granted for a videotape entitled *Bernie Fisher, Everyday Hero,* produced by Kelly Fisher and Nathan Fisher, copyright 2001 KBYU Television,[1] and subsequently reviewed and approved by Paco, Denny, and Luke.

FRANCISCO "PACO" VAZQUEZ

The last transmission that made it through my damaged radio was to warn Bernie about a fixed enemy gun that was in position to really cause us a lot of grief. He seemed pretty distracted and said, "Why don't you see if you can take it out?" So I left the crash area, engaged the anti-aircraft gun battery, and destroyed it.

When the pilot crashed on the Ashau runway and the pilot came out running through the flames, it looked like he

1. For a copy, please consult www.creativeworks.byu.edu or call 1–800–962–8061. Used with permission.

was probably burned severely. My only thought was that maybe we could cover a helicopter to drop down and bring him out. I didn't hear Bernie say he was going to go down because my radios had failed.

When I realized that Bernie was turning his airplane around with his landing gear extended, I thought that his airplane had been damaged and he was also going to try to land, and then we'd have two airplanes down there. I have to be honest and tell you that at no time had the thought crossed my mind that he was going to land and pick that man up. It was with a great sigh of relief that I watched him apply power and go around after the first approach, and then I understood that first and foremost, his airplane was okay and he was okay. He was still flying. But then the realization came that he was going to land and attempt a rescue. At the moment I did not have time to examine that concept. I simply had to support my leader—that's what I had to do, and that's what I did. The thinking about what he did came later, and it has taken me years to fully understand the magnitude of his action.

After thinking about it for all those years, off and on, it has changed my outlook on the true nature of heroism. From the time I was a boy, my heroes were Batman and Captain Marvel and the cowboys on the screen, but of course these were make-believe heroes. After Ashau, I realized that nobody teaches you about real-life heroes. You have to learn that from the experiences of a lifetime. Until you've seen one in action and you understand that this is real and not a movie, and that it's coming out okay only because of the skill and daring and courage of this man, this one man running the operation, only then do you gain a different appreciation of heroism.

The thing that distinguishes heroes is that they'll put something dear of theirs on the line. They'll put it at risk for no real reward except that their act is going to—in one way or another—result in a good outcome for someone else. It may be the saving of a life. It may be that the hero fails in the sense that he comes very close but doesn't save that life. But still, that is the essence. He is doing something for someone else at a risk to his own person or his own well-being.

Probably the most anxious and heroic moment at Ashau was when Bernie was sitting on the runway with the canopy open while Jump Myers was running toward the airplane. Bernie was left sitting still, and the airplane was not moving, and that was the hardest moment for me personally because he was my leader. When you're flying, you can take evasive action. But he was sitting on the runway, and they were shooting at him. The man who was running didn't seem to be running very fast. I'm sure he was running as fast as he could, but as far I was concerned, he was just walking. And then Bernie was ready to get out of the airplane to get him. That was the moment when Bernie risked everything.

I came to realize that there are different levels of heroes. I was fortunate to have been associated with the highest level. It is a real-life thing that you feel privileged to have observed firsthand.

DENNY HAGUE

For me the story of the rescue starts the night before when Bernie returned from his Silver Star mission. Even though it was late, we all gathered in his hooch to ask questions about the camp and about the problems the Special Forces were having up there. It was pretty common for pilots to try to figure out the scene of a battle. I can remember thinking that Bernie and his wingman had given those guys another breath of life to make it through the night—also that he was very, very brave. What a wonderful mission they had done—the people on the ground were in heavy, heavy distress, and so he got those airplanes in there with ammo and food. We were interested in it because those efforts were life-saving, and that's what we were there for, even though it sounded like in spite of the support it wasn't going to work out very well for the people up there.

After we got a divert to Ashau the next morning, we arrived at about the same time as some F-4 jet fighters, and even though they weren't suited to close ground support, they just felt like they had to do something. So they streaked through the valley, even though it was suicidal at their speed. I mean, they were smoking, because they had to do something to help that camp. That's how desperately we all wanted to help the men on the ground.

After the F-4s exited the area, Bernie found a hole in the clouds that he recognized from the day before. It's almost impossible to do that, but somehow he could always find a hole and get in. So he gave us a fix on that, and we started back to the point. Bernie, Paco, Jump, and Hubie showed up almost simultaneously with our arrival. There was not going to be room for six airplanes down in that little valley, so Bernie said, "All right, we'll go down, and Luke, you and Denny hang. Why don't you orbit up there, and we'll call you down when we need you."

That sounded like a good idea. At that point, Luke and I had no idea about the anti-aircraft batteries, but as soon as they went into the hole, we started hearing the radio chatter about the weapons fire they were encountering. The next thing we saw was Hubie coming out with his canopy shot away. Then there was the talk about Jump getting shot down, and we started down there and immediately came under fire. Some of the anti-aircraft guns were higher than we were. I don't think that was by accident; it was by design. We were just flying down a tube. Someone said it was like flying inside Yankee Stadium, and everybody in the cheap seats had guns.

During the rescue itself, there were a couple of times that we were wondering what was going to happen next. You know, Luke is on fire, he's lost his hydraulics, he's out of ammunition, yet he decides to stay and fight. Some pilots asked Paco and me once if we would have ever thought of landing and picking up Jump. I don't know the answer. It's not that we wouldn't try to rescue him—it's that the odds were so stacked against such a thing that I don't think we ever thought of it as an option in the circumstance. I would hope that it wasn't by cowardice—it was just that the idea of a fixed-wing aircraft landing would have never passed our brain as an option.

But Bernie did think of it, which is what sets him apart. When the time came, we did our best to support him. While he was on the ground, most of the enemy fire was coming from the east side, and that's where we were trying to keep the bad guys away. We were literally doing extreme things, such as skid the airplanes, which means set on the rudders so the nose would be pointed in one direction, and when you pulled off and stopped on the rudders it would look like the airplane was going to turn one way, but it would turn the other. We were doing just about everything we could not to be a target.

After Luke got hit, we continued our strafing runs, even though we were both Winchester. When Bernie made it up and out, we headed straight for Da Nang to get Luke back to safety.

And that's pretty much the story. It was hard to believe I actually got to see that, and as we've talked about it through the years, we all agree that we could not have planned it and had it succeed—all the things that had to come together there, just to make it work. It was just meant to be. The Lord kind of points you in the direction, and he heard our prayers that day.

Jon Lucas (Luke)

The Medal of Honor is the highest decoration for bravery in the United States. The bar on the top of the medal says "Valor," a word that comes from the French. It means strength to commit, strength to sustain, strength to do what has to be done to risk one's life above and beyond the call of duty, and that's what Bernie did. Now he's recognized wherever he goes, and he's really one of the few surviving recipients who goes around and talks to people. And so he has done a great deal for the *esprit de corps* of the entire Air Force. I'm sure he affects other services the same way, because the A-1E pilots had somewhat of a distinction in the fact that we did close-air support work for the Army.

Bernie was a strong pilot, obviously gifted in flying airplanes. He just had a natural set of hands for it. He was quiet and reserved. In my career, I've worked with a very diversified group of fighter pilots who represent all nationalities, beliefs, and all kinds of personalities. My experience has generally been that the flamboyant ones who "wrist watch"[2] fight at the bars and brag about their accomplishments are never there for you. When the going gets tough and you're in a knife fight at 20,000 feet, it's the guys like Bernie that are the ones you can count on.

Heroes to me are people who, when thing get really bad, they get really good. Bernie went in to rescue Jump without even knowing who he was—he just knew that an aviator was down and burning. His loyalty was to the uniform and to the family—the Air Force family. Teamwork was also important. In the rescue at Ashau, Bernie knew he could depend on the guys around him. He paid us the highest accolade that anybody could ever pay another pilot when he said, "They were real cool characters, and they hit what they were shooting at." He knew we would be there for him, and we were. We didn't take a vote, we didn't say, "What do you guys think?" When he said, "I'm going to land," we just said to ourselves, "Okay, what do we have to do here?" If you tried to script it, to make a movie out of it, everybody would say you were crazy—it couldn't happen. And it probably couldn't if you planned it. When I rolled out of the valley, I just didn't believe it. I was

2. Fighter pilots using both hands to describe aircraft performing aerial combat maneuvers.

pretty convinced that I would die in that valley. But that didn't change what had to be done.

I wasn't even thinking about whether we could pull it off, because the odds seemed insurmountable to have him be able to land and get off that runway without being shot down. My biggest fear was that after he pulled Jump into the airplane and was taxiing back down the runway to turn around that he would just get hammered on takeoff. That's why we spaced ourselves the way we did, and it worked out perfectly. But nobody had practiced it, nobody had talked about it, nobody had ever thought about it—it just happened. It comes from discipline and training.

I've always believed that bravery is nothing more than a control of your fear. If you can control your fear, then you're probably perceived and seen as brave. I don't think anybody I've ever known that was considered a hero actually considered himself to be a hero. They did what they had to do.

In Ashau it was nothing more than control of fear. I mean, any one of us had an excuse to leave. Paco could have left because he had no communication. Denny could have left because I was on fire, and he said, "You need to get out of here." He was concerned about me and as my wingman could have left if I had. I could have simply said, "I'm on fire" and left. But I don't think the thought of leaving ever entered our minds. Even if it did, I don't think any of us ever considered exercising that option. We controlled the fear and made it out.

Perhaps that's the difference between a movie hero and real-life hero. In combat nobody can say, "Cut!" The fight just goes on.

APPENDIX B

VIETNAM FLIGHT PROTOCOL

In my first days in Vietnam, I was assigned as a flight instructor to Vietnamese students. Military missions are flown with precise planning to destroy a predetermined target following a specific protocol to assure order in the field of combat. Here is a step-by-step listing of a typical training mission:

Each night we'd get a posting for the next day's activities. The next day, we'd arrive at the briefing area approximately one and a half hours before flight time. The containment area we lived in was just to the side of the airfield, so it was a quick walk to the support buildings, where we'd change into our flight clothes and then go into Operations to wait for the briefing.

First up was a senior squadron officer to brief us on the nature of the mission and our objectives. If the mission was to unfamiliar territory, he'd provide details on the area, including geography, battlefield conditions, location of friendly and hostile forces, and so on.

Next was a weather briefing, customized to expected conditions based on time of day and terrain. Fog is more dangerous in the mountains, for example, than on an open plain.

On training missions, they assigned us our Vietnamese students, providing time for individual discussions with the students, once the formal briefing was complete, to review maps of the area and to discuss the type of practice we'd do for the day. The flight instructor went into very specific detail so the students could picture everything clearly in their minds. Most of the time, we'd practice formation flying or practice simulated hard bomb runs.

Each squadron had its own call sign. I was assigned to "Hobo," while one of our companion squadrons was "Surf." Rescue missions were identified as a "Sandy." You'd use the call sign to identify yourself when communicating by radio.

Once the classroom work was completed, a truck transported us to the flight line, where we'd be issued an M-16 rifle to store in the aircraft and an individual handgun to carry on our person. A lot of the pilots liked to carry a .45-caliber weapon, but I preferred a .38 special.

The transport truck then took us to pick up a parachute and finally to our specific aircraft to complete a preflight checklist. We'd walk around looking for any damage or mechanical flaws that could cause a problem in flight and, if satisfied that the aircraft was okay, we'd sign a form 781, which essentially said, "I accept responsibility for this aircraft, recognizing that maintenance has done a complete check and repair before releasing it to me."

Next we would strap on our parachutes, board the aircraft, and settle back into the seat (which was designed with a cavity in the back to accommodate the parachute). The student strapped in on the left side.

The world looked a little different once the canopy was closed, since it had a strong blue tint on the windows to cut down on glare and keep out some of the stifling heat of the sun.

A typical training mission required us to fly south from Bien Hoa toward the radio beacon at the large airfield at Tan Son Nhut, then onto a practice target outside of the Saigon area. When the appointed time arrived to check in, we'd sit in the airplane waiting for the flight leader to check in on the preassigned ground-radio frequency. He'd speak into the microphone of his helmet, "Hobo flight, check in." We'd answer back "Hobo 51, all clear," "Hobo 52, clear," and so on, until all aircraft had reported ready. At precisely the appointed time, he'd give the signal for us to start the engines, and then we'd each check in with the tower for permission to taxi out to the runway. The tower controls all aircraft at the base, including those on the ground, to prevent confusion.

Just before pulling onto the runway, we'd stop the aircraft for the ground crew to complete a "last chance check" to look for oil leaks, hydraulic leaks, or an abnormal sound to the engine. If something was wrong, they'd pull us out with instructions to return to the hangar.

Once all the aircraft in the flight were cleared, the

controller would instruct us to change from ground frequency to a designated air frequency, with a command such as "Let's go to 243.0, Hobo 51, 52, 53, and 54," and then we'd check in with the tower on the new frequency, individually reporting, "Tower, this, is Hobo 51—we're ready for the active." When the field was clear, the tower would respond, "Hobo 5-1, taxi into position and hold."

We usually flew in two aircraft formations, but up to four could line up at the same time. Once in position, each aircraft completed a final check with the tower, then looked to the lead aircraft for the pilot to make a circling motion with his finger, which means "Wind them up!" The other pilots would advance the power while holding the aircraft in position with the brakes.

On a mission without ordnance, all aircraft can take off simultaneously in a preassigned formation. With ordnance, each aircraft takes off one-by-one, separated by ten-second intervals. That allows a troubled aircraft to alert those that are scheduled to follow to hold in position until the problem is resolved. The reason for this procedure is that a heavily loaded aircraft under full acceleration simply can't stop when it reaches takeoff velocity, so it's up to the person following to avoid a collision. On one occasion, I was flying wing to the operations officer flying the lead. He accelerated down the field with a full load of ordnance, and as he lifted off and rotated, his gun-cover doors accidentally opened, which immediately killed his flying speed. He should have alerted me as to what was happening, but he was too busy concentrating on the aircraft to give warning. I took off ten seconds later with a full load of ordnance, probably 8,000 pounds, and I pushed the engine right to the firewall with all she'd take. By the time I saw he was in trouble, there was simply no way I could stop. He didn't clear far enough off the side of the runway to avoid a near hit, and I came up right under his wingtip. We probably missed each other by less than a few feet. With that much ordnance on the two aircraft, a collision would almost certainly have proved fatal to both of us. Once airborne, we kind of got our bearings together, and he returned to base while another aircraft came up to join me.

Once the flight leader was satisfied that everything looked okay, he nodded his head, tipped it back, then moved it forward again sharply as a visual order to the other pilots to release their brakes. The aircraft lurched ahead under full power. It's one of the most beautiful sights in the world to see four aircraft reach lift-off velocity at precisely the same moment. As the wheels left the ground, everyone rotated in the same direction, staying in precise formation on a predetermined flight path to leave the area.

Oftentimes the weather conditions required the formation to take off in the opposite direction of the mission, since we always took off into the wind to get maximum lift. On a sequenced takeoff, the procedure called for the lead aircraft, once airborne, to fly ahead for twenty seconds, then execute a 180-degree turn and proceed in the new direction at a reduced airspeed so the wingman can catch up and slide into formation.

All of this was pretty nerve-wracking for our students, but that's why we were there—to give them instructions as necessary and to help them orient their thinking to flight plan. Combat flying can be quite confusing, and you have to keep track of all the helicopters in the area, other fixed-wing aircraft, and so on. It took real concentration to fly where you were supposed to go without interfering with other aircraft.

At the conclusion of the mission, each aircraft checked in with ground control for permission to enter a landing pattern that brought everyone down in an orderly fashion. You then taxied to the hangar, reported any damage or maintenance problems to the ground chief, and then changed out of your flight gear. The last step was to debrief the mission to provide up-to-the-minute intelligence on battlefield conditions.

APPENDIX C

A BRIEF HISTORY OF VIETNAM AND THE WAR

By Jerry Borrowman

VIETNAM IS AN ANCIENT COUNTRY in Southeast Asia that enjoyed little international notice until America went to war there in 1965. With more than 1,800 miles of coastline forming its eastern boundary on the South China Sea, the country is shaped like a long and narrow letter S. It's just 35 miles across at its narrowest point, 360 miles at its widest point in the north, and 240 miles in the south. Vietnam's total land mass is roughly the size of the state of New Mexico but with a coastline 50 percent longer than California, Oregon, and Washington combined. This unique geography contributed to Vietnam's partitions into north and south for extended periods during the past 2,000 years.

The most prominent physical features of Vietnam are the Annamese and Cordillera mountain ranges that form a spine snaking down its western borders with neighboring Laos and

Cambodia. Two great rivers provide nourishment to its 65 million inhabitants and form great flood-plain deltas where food can be grown. The Red River in the north passes through Hanoi, while the Mekong River in the south passes through Saigon (now Ho Chi Minh City).

In retrospect, it's easy to figure out why the United States was taking on such an overwhelming challenge in attempting to resist the Vietnamese in their desire for reunification of their country. For example, in 60 B.C., the Chinese managed to subjugate the Viet people but spent the next 1,000 years in a never-ending battle to suppress their constant rebellions and desire for independence. The Chinese finally gave up in exhaustion in A.D. 939 when the Vietnamese overwhelmed their far more numerous conquerors from the north. The Viets accomplished this by perfecting the art of guerilla warfare, in which small parties strike out unexpectedly against a military or civilian target, then quickly withdraw into the jungle to hide from their pursuers. In spite of massive efforts at retaliation, these guerilla fighters were able to hunker down and suffered remarkably few casualties compared to the damage they inflicted on their enemy, who had to operate in the open.

After separation from China, two Viet countries operated independently, Tonkin in the north and Cochinchina in the south. The Vietnamese maintained this independence for nearly 900 years before political turmoil in the mid-1800s provided Imperial French forces an opportunity to intervene with superior military force so France could take advantage of the area's natural resources. Eventually, France dominated the entire region, combining Vietnam, Laos, and Cambodia into French Indochina. These new colonies and protectorates were certainly profitable for France economically, but France had its hands full trying to keep order in the region, since strong revolutionary and nationalist movements were constantly struggling for self-rule. French Indochina fell to the Japanese in World War II, but soon after the war, a dynamic young leader named Ho Chi Minh proclaimed Vietnamese independence and the creation of the new Democratic Republic of Vietnam. It was Ho Chi Minh's belief that Vietnam should be free to pursue its own identity and choose its own government, citing the United States Declaration of Independence in the speech he gave establishing the rights of the Vietnamese to self-rule.

France was not impressed and prepared for war to reassert control in their colonial territory. This forced the "Viet Minh," as Ho Chi Minh's followers were called, to once again adopt the ancient practice of guerilla warfare in a calculated effort to make life intolerable for the French. This strategy required incredible patience on the part of the Vietnamese, but they were willing to take their time in order to wear the French down. The French were persistent, but it didn't seem to matter how much traditional military force the French brought to bear; the Viet Minh simply sloughed it off and kept going. By always maintaining the element of surprise, the Viet Minh could make their attack, then simply slip out of view to hide and wait for another opportunity. For seven and a half years the French fought to reestablish French Indochina.

Finally, in 1954, the French gave up their control over Vietnam, worn out by the guerilla strategy of attrition, just as the Chinese had done a millennium earlier. At a peace conference in Geneva, Switzerland, it was determined that Vietnam would be divided into two countries, with North Vietnam organized as communists under Ho Chi Minh, while South Vietnam would operate as a republic under the initial presidency of Ngo Dinh Diem. The dividing line was the seventeenth parallel, where the land is very narrow between the ocean and the mountains. This choice of a dividing line gave North and South Vietnam roughly the same borders as ancient Tonkin and Cochinchina. Washing their hands of their former colonies, the French withdrew, and the two countries attempted to establish themselves as independent nations.

Almost immediately, the North Vietnamese started agitating for unification of the two countries and initiated the practice of sending raiding parties into areas of South Vietnam to stir up the local population to rebellion and to attack military installations. These North Vietnamese guerillas and South Vietnamese sympathizers were called "Viet Cong." To carry out their surreptitious raids, they often crossed into neighboring Laos and Cambodia, where they could hide until ready to strike. This also meant they could move into position all along the western boundary of South Vietnam in order to launch an attack against the Army of the Republic of Vietnam (ARVN) from the north, west, and southwest. By the early 1960s, the Viet Cong and regular army units of the Democratic Republic of Vietnam (DRV) posed a genuine threat to the viability of the government of South Vietnam. A large patchwork of communist-occupied territory began to consume ever-increasing amounts of land in South Vietnam, and by 1965 a great deal of the fertile Mekong Delta, as well as much of the coastline, had fallen under communist control.

One of the reasons they enjoyed success in recruiting the local civilian population was that the "democratic" government of the south was really despotic in nature and generally unpopular with its own people. While it may be that many South Vietnamese were uncertain as to whether they'd like to unify with the North, most were ready for a change of government but saw no opportunity to bring about a legitimate change through the ballot box. So they joined the Viet Cong in their armed agitation.

Enter the United States. In the early 1960s, the premier of the Union of Soviet Socialist Republics (USSR), Nikita Khrushchev, had pounded his shoe on the podium of the United Nations, promising to bury the capitalist democracies of the West in the "ash heap" of history. With many of the poorer nations of the world lining up with the communist superpowers, Russia and China, the United States was concerned that the "red plague" of communism would continue to spread throughout the Asian continent. A decade earlier, a very costly war had been fought in Korea to prevent the spread of Chinese communism into the south, and now it appeared that a similar battle was needed to keep South Vietnam free of Soviet domination. Thus, the United States took an interest in propping up the supposedly democratic government in South Vietnam, seeing this as an opportunity to stop the domino effect that threatened to topple the fledgling democracies in that part of the world. Nearly 16,000 U.S. military advisers had been active in South Vietnam since

1961, and the United States poured more than 400 million dollars into the effort to bolster the ARVN.

The year 1963 turned out to be pivotal for the fate of South Vietnam. President Diem, a Catholic, made the wildly unpopular decision to ban the flying of the Buddhist flag, which prompted a number of Buddhist priests to publicly immolate (burn) themselves to death in protest. The public furor and sympathy for the Buddhists emboldened the Viet Cong to attack even more vigorously, and many in the army deserted to join the Viet Cong. In that same year President Diem was assassinated, and a military junta assumed control. Also in that year, President John F. Kennedy was assassinated in Texas, leaving the Vietnam issue to Lyndon B. Johnson to deal with.

As 1964 progressed, the political instability in South Vietnam escalated, with frequent coups and government reorganizations. The Buddhists kept up their pressure on public opinion, and Viet Cong terrorist attacks against American installations increased in tempo and ferocity. In the absence of outside intervention, it was becoming obvious that the government of South Vietnam would soon fall to communist control.

In August 1964, it was reported that North Vietnamese gun ships had attacked the U.S.S. *Maddox*, a destroyer cruising in the Gulf of Tonkin near Hanoi. Two days later, the *Maddox* was again attacked, along with another U.S. Navy ship, and together they returned fire, sinking two North Vietnamese vessels. This action on the part of the North Vietnamese outraged the U.S. Congress, which passed the "Tonkin Resolution," authorizing the president to use force to protect United States interests in the area. Some people believe the forays by the *Maddox* were specifically designed to provoke the North Vietnamese so the United States would have a pretext for escalating the level of violence in the area.

Soon, U.S. aircraft were flying bombing raids into North Vietnamese territory, as well as into neighboring Laos to bomb the Ho Chi Minh Trail, the major supply artery for the Viet Cong from the north. In early 1965, President Johnson proposed peace discussions to try to bring to pass a nonmilitary solution to the problem, but he was rebuffed by the North Vietnamese (who undoubtedly saw their position as one of increasing strength). In June 1965 a ten-member military junta assumed control of South Vietnam under the leadership of Air Force Commander Vice-Marshal Nguyen Cao Ky, who served as premier. While not popular with the citizens, this new government did establish civil control of South Vietnam, eventually placating many of the Buddhist's most urgent demands.

While a precise moment can't be assigned to when the United States was officially at war in Vietnam (since the only authorizing legislation was the Bay of Tonkin resolution), 1965 was clearly the point when hostilities increased beyond the adviser role into active fighting on the part of regular U.S. military personnel. By midyear the United States had more than 50,000 troops on active duty, supported by a much smaller contingent from South Korea, Australia, and New Zealand. Another 100,000 U.S. troops were transferred to South Vietnam in time for the rainy season. This year also marked the first time the Viet Cong fought out in the open rather than using strictly guerilla tactics. By 1968, more than

500,000 American troops were serving in Vietnam on active assignment. More than 2,500,000 U.S. military personnel would rotate in and out of the combat area in the course of eight years from 1965 to 1973.

While the American combatants enjoyed some battlefield successes, they were almost always restrained in their ability to wage all-out war because of political considerations. For example, many believe that the only way America and South Vietnam could have prevailed was to launch a massive preemptive strike against the north right at the beginning of the war. Unfortunately, experience in Korea showed that when the Americans pressed their advantage after turning back the North Korean troops, who had occupied much of South Korea, the Chinese sent in their troops to protect their border with North Korea. It was believed that the Chinese would be equally intolerant of an American advance into North Vietnam (which shared its northern border with China), and the last thing the government of the United States wanted was to be drawn into direct conflict with either the U.S.S.R. or China. The threat of nuclear engagement, which was shown to be very real with the Cuban Missile Crisis, made it politically intolerable for an administration to bring the United States into direct conflict with another nuclear power. That's why wars were fought through surrogates, like South Vietnam. So instead, the war escalated slowly in half measures, in which ground gained one day was given up the next, only to be retaken on a later offensive.

Politically, the war was a nightmare for President Johnson, since many in the United States failed to see how our interests were directly threatened. Also, the continuing unpopularity of the repressive Ky government in the south meant we were defending a government that wasn't supported by its own people. So much for the idea of supporting democracy. President Johnson quickly felt the sting of popular opinion and made a number of offers to negotiate a settlement in December 1965 and 1966, but once again the North Vietnamese failed to respond. To increase pressure, the United States began bombing North Vietnamese military installations in Hanoi and Haiphong (the largest harbor in the north), but this failed to have the hoped-for effect.

In January 1968, the North Vietnamese launched a major military offensive during Tet, the Vietnamese Lunar New Year holiday, which met with a great deal of success. By March, President Johnson was in real trouble politically, so he ordered a cessation of hostile bombing of North Vietnam in another attempt to lure them to the bargaining table. Peace talks began in Paris in May but made little progress on any substantive issues, and the war went on. President Johnson eventually announced that he would not seek or accept reelection, fearful that he would be the only president in American history to preside over a losing war. The problem then fell to Richard Nixon, who also tried both the carrot and the stick approach to diplomacy by periodically increasing military activity (including surreptitious raids on Cambodia and Laos to disrupt communist supply lines to the south), along with periods of reduced activity.

Militarily, the war was also a living nightmare for the soldiers serving on the ground in Vietnam, since it was never clear who the enemy was. With the Viet Cong made up of both North Vietnamese agitators and South Vietnamese sympathizers, it was impossible to be certain that the smiling South Vietnamese citizen approaching in a friendly manner wasn't about to blow you or your buddy up the moment you got within range. The constant harassment was wearing on our troops, and the policy of rotating in and rotating out after a specified number of service hours were accumulated meant that the battlefield camaraderie that bolstered American troops in World War II was often nonexistent. On any particular day, a U.S. unit might consist of a handful of experienced soldiers, who were often calloused by their combat experience, as well as a bunch of new, inexperienced troops, who could easily put the entire unit at risk by making a mistake. All this uncertainty came together in a mass execution of villagers at My Lai, creating a blight on the record of the field commanders and an international outrage that further inflamed antiwar sentiments at home and abroad.

One of the most interesting developments of the Vietnam War was the remarkable synergy that developed between the U.S. Air Force and the troops on the ground. Helicopters were used to quickly move the "air artillery" to hot points where they could intervene in a battle, as well as to extract soldiers who came under fire or needed medical evacuation. Military aircraft also became skilled in precision bombing and strafing to support American and South Vietnamese ground troops with sophisticated surface-to-air communications giving precise guidance to where support was needed.

Politically, the war was causing ever-deeper problems at home in America, and it became imperative for President

Nixon and Secretary of State Henry Kissinger to bring about an end to the war. Nixon came up with the idea of the "Vietnamization" of the war, which meant that American troops would be withdrawn while ARVN units were strengthened. This began in 1969, and by 1971 less than 200,000 American troops remained in the country.

Still, the U.S. kept up military pressure, primarily through heavy airstrikes against the north, through 1972. During this time, Kissinger conducted a series of secret negotiations in Paris that ended with the signing of a cease-fire on January 27, 1973, by the United States, South Vietnam, and North Vietnam. The treaty called for the continuing independence of both North and South Vietnam, but once the United States was out of the way, fighting started up again, with both sides claiming violations of the truce. A second cease-fire was signed in June 1973, but the fighting continued through the rest of 1973 and all of 1974. In early 1975, the North Vietnamese began a sustained and withering attack that began to gobble up South Vietnamese cities. It soon became apparent that nothing could stop the rout, as more and more ARVN units surrendered and joined the Viet Cong. In April 1975, all remaining U.S. citizens were airlifted out of South Vietnam, along with many thousands of South Vietnamese citizens who had supported the United States and whose lives would be at risk if they were captured by the North Vietnamese. In a dramatic ending that had the U.S. embassy surrounded by Viet Cong, the last of the South Vietnamese citizens that could possibly be lifted off the roof of the embassy were transported out to U.S. aircraft carriers as the government of South Vietnam collapsed. An official surrender was signed on April 30, 1975.

In the months and years that followed, many thousands more made their way out of Vietnam in small sampans and other boats, with more than 130,000 South Vietnamese eventually given asylum in the United States.

As the war ended, America tallied the cost in American lives and injuries. With 371,825 casualties, including 47,343 combat deaths, Vietnam was the third most costly war in American history, after the Civil War and World War II (there were more combat deaths in World War I but fewer overall casualties).

The Vietnam War was also very costly in its impact on the American political system, as well as on the emotional lives of many of the men and women who served there—particularly the soldiers who served on the ground.

America entered the war for two reasons—first, out of a sincere desire to help a fledgling democracy, and, second, to contain the spread of communism. The second fear proved unfounded, since virtually no other countries in Southeast Asia adopted the communist model after the Vietnam War. Perhaps that was simply the consequence of the decline of the U.S.S.R., or in part because of the effort America made in Vietnam. At any rate, it was a sound military defeat for a country that had never before been beaten on the field of battle, and its legacy will take many years to fully assess.

REFERENCES

Addington, Larry H. *America's War in Vietnam: A Short Narrative History.* Bloomington, Ind.: Indiana University Press, 2000.

Vietnam War. Compton's Interactive Encyclopedia. SoftKey Multimedia, 1996.

Vietnam National Administration of Tourism. www.vietnamtourism.com. Address: 80 Quan Su Hanoi, Vietnam. Telephone 84–4–9421061/8224714.

AUTHOR'S NOTE

By Jerry Borrowman

Working with Bernie Fisher on this book has been a particularly rewarding experience. I was a bit intimidated, at first, to work with an authentic American hero. What one finds in Bernie, however, is a person who is at once extremely humble and self-deprecating while confident and assured about his status. He always finds reasons to compliment other people and sincerely enjoys their accomplishments.

Probably the thing I've come to appreciate most is how he and his family accept life as it comes. In spite of his Parkinson's disease, Bernie works actively on his farm, attends Air Force and community functions when his schedule allows, and stays active in his church. He's extremely kind and patient with Realla's disability, always making sure I took time to go into her room to say hello when I visited. In spite of the difficulty of moving her around, Bernie, along with the family members who assist in her care, take her out each week to get her hair done, to church each Sunday, and to special events as they become available. Together they continue to have as full and rewarding a life as possible.

Bernie is a person who makes things look easy—so much so that his skill is a little deceptive, and one can overlook the precision he brings to a task. Two incidents helped me understand why he is so effective. I'd stopped at his farm on my way to a meeting in McCall, Idaho, hoping we could sit down and sign our publishing agreement. When it was time to leave, he walked me out to my rental car. Just as I was about to get in and start on a two-hour drive up a one-lane highway through remote areas, Bernie stopped me and said, "What's this?" pointing to the passenger side rear wheel on my rental car. I was horrified to find that three of the five lug nuts were missing, and the fourth was about to fall off. Bernie had done the equivalent of a preflight checklist on the car and discovered a potentially fatal problem. In all my life I've never done a walkaround, yet apparently he does that every time he operates something mechanical. He tightened the fourth lug nut, and I drove carefully back to the Boise airport to trade the car in for another.

The second incident happened after we finished the book and as I was doing research for a World War I novel I planned to write. I'd decided to make one of my characters a fighter pilot, but I couldn't figure out how the various controls worked in a World War I era airplane. So I asked Bernie if he knew any aero clubs that might have an open seat bi-plane that I could study. "My neighbor, Chuck Jopson, has a restored 1939 bi-plane," he replied casually. I was astonished—who else in the world could you ask a question like that of and expect that kind of an answer? At my request Bernie arranged for me to see the airplane on my next trip up to Boise. Chuck and his wife, Leanne, were very kind and let me sit in the airplane and study the controls, watching how the ailerons, elevators, and rudder work. It was an invaluable experience for my writing. Unfortunately, the aircraft was in maintenance, so I couldn't go flying in it.

Two months later, however, I had a two-hour window, and Chuck agreed to leave work early to take me up. When we arrived, Bernie drove over and helped us walk the airplane out of its hangar. I was so excited I could hardly stand it. Chuck helped me get strapped in; then he said from the back seat, using the intercom in the headset, "I hope I can get this started—sometimes it's kind of difficult." My heart was pounding, because I wanted to go up so badly. I saw one of the gauges in front of me drop down to zero, and Chuck said, "Oh, no, I left the switch open, and the battery is dead." My heart sank. As we started to get out, Bernie said from the ground, "What's the matter?" Chuck explained the problem, and Bernie replied, "Why can't we jump-start it?" Chuck looked a bit perplexed; then he explained that the battery was behind a panel that had six or seven screws that secured it. Once the plane started, if it worked, Chuck would have to stay in the cockpit. "Can you handle the jumper cables and the panel?" he asked Bernie. "Sure," Bernie said. So, we hooked up the aircraft to one of the cars, and as the engine sputtered to life with a black cloud of smoke, Bernie moved in, easily removed the cables, secured the panel, and gave us an "all clear" sign. If the trembling from his Parkinson's disease made it a challenge, he didn't show any sign of it. For my part, flying with Chuck was the experience of a lifetime, made possible by my friendship with Bernie.

That's the kind of person Bernie Fisher is—someone who will do anything to help you out if it's in his power, and he always seems so pleased when people call or stop by. It's an honor to have him as a friend.